PROCLAMATION COMMENTARIES

• The Old Testament
Witnesses for Preaching

Foster R. McCurley, *Editor*

THE PSALMS, JOB

Roland E. Murphy, *O. Carm.*

FORTRESS PRESS   Philadelphia, Pennsylvania

To

David Murphy

Library of Congress Cataloging in Publication Data
Murphy, Roland Edmund, 1917–
    The Psalms, Job.
    (Proclamation commentaries)
    Bibliography: p.
    Includes index.
    1.   Bible.   O.T. Psalms—Commentaries.   2.   Bible.
O.T.   Job—Commentaries.   I.   Title.
BS1430.3.M87   223'.1'07   77-78637
ISBN 0-8006-0588-8

6442E77   Printed in U.S.A.   1-588

CONTENTS

EDITOR'S FOREWORD

This present volume introduces *Proclamation Commentaries–The Old Testament Witnesses for Preaching*. Like its New Testament counterpart, this series is not intended to replace traditional commentaries which analyze books of the Bible pericope by pericope or verse by verse. This six-volume series attempts to provide background material on selected Old Testament books which, among other things, will assist the reader in using *Proclamation: Aids for Interpreting the Lessons of the Church Year*. Material offered in these volumes will consist of theological themes from various witnesses or theologians out of Israel's believing community. It is our expectation that this approach—examining characteristic themes and motifs—will enable the modern interpreter to comprehend more clearly and fully a particular pericope which contains or alludes to such a subject. In order to give appropriate emphasis to such issues in the brief form of these volumes, the authors will present the results, rather than the detailed arguments, of contemporary scholarship.

On the basis of its concern to address the specific tasks of preaching and teaching the word of God to audiences today, this commentary series will stress the theological dilemmas which Old Testament Israel faced and to which her witnesses responded. Accordingly, the historical and political details of Israel's life and that of her ancient Near Eastern neighbors will be left to other books. Selected for discussion here will be those incidents and issues in Israel's history which have a direct relationship to the theological problems and responses in her existence. Since the word of God is always addressed to specific and concrete situations in the life of people, the motifs and themes in these commentaries will be directed to those selected situations which best exemplify a certain witness's theology.

This initial volume, *The Psalms, Job,* might by its very subject matter seem to belie the intention of the series. The Book of Psalms is not preaching in a strict sense; it is not a collection of sermons addressed to specific historical situations—as are the prophetic books. Neither is it a continuing narrative in which episodes are arranged in such a way that they present theology as story. The Psalter is a collection of various types of hymns, the arrangement of which seems rather arbitrary. And yet Professor Roland Murphy demonstrates throughout the first part of this volume that even the task of describing a particular psalm according to its literary type brings about a confrontation between modern reader and ancient witness on which one can build a theology of the Psalter and evaluate the potential of the Psalms for proclamation today.

It is this classification of psalms according to various literary types or genre that lies at the heart of modern psalm study. Ever since the pioneering work of Hermann Gunkel at the beginning of this century on the form–critical approach to the psalms, scholars have been busy classifying psalms according to their content, structure, and use in Israel's worship. Several renowned scholars have attempted to emphasize one or another festival in Israel's worship in which many psalms served particular cultic functions. Gunkel's student, the Scandinavian scholar Sigmund Mowinckel, sought to interpret many psalms on the basis of a New Year festival, which in his own reconstruction is closely akin to the Babylonian *akitu.* Artur Weiser posits a covenant renewal festival as the basis for a multitude of psalms. Hans Joachim Kraus interprets a number of psalms according to a royal Zion festival.

No matter which interpreter one chooses to follow, the important feature of this scholarly debate is that the psalms had a particular use in the worship life of ancient Israel. In this volume Roland Murphy succinctly identifies the various classifications of psalms and discusses their roles as a means of deriving theological issues. In addition, the author employs the same literary types in order to reach into our own personal and corporate worship with a fresh and profound treatment of prayer.

Likewise the Book of Job is not preaching in the strict sense. Along with Proverbs and Ecclesiastes, Job is designated as a wisdom book. Wisdom tends to be didactic rather than kerygmatic. It takes varied forms and is classified further as optimistic wisdom, pessimistic wisdom, old wisdom, theological wisdom, court wisdom, clan wisdom, and so on. Detailed studies on the nature of the various types of wisdom and its role in the Old Testament include, above all, Gerhard von Rad, *Wisdom in Israel* (Nashville: Abingdon, 1972), William McKane, *Proverbs.* The Old Testament Library, (Philadelphia: Westminster, 1970), and the collected essays in Martin Noth and D. Winton Thomas, eds. *Wisdom in Israel and in the Ancient Near East* (Leiden: E. J. Brill, 1960).

The issue in the Book of Job is the battle between optimistic wisdom and pessimistic wisdom. The optimistic variety, best illustrated in the Book of Proverbs, taught the simple doctrine that the good are rewarded and the wicked are punished. Pessimistic wisdom is simply a reaction to that doctrine which in reality does not hold true. Both types are present in the Book of Job: optimism is the position of Job's friends; pessimism (reaction) is clearly the viewpoint of the author or redactor of the book. A modern preacher must exercise caution, therefore, in selecting a piece of the book as a sermon text. A given set of verses might in fact represent a theological position which is contrary to the theology of the Book of Job as a whole and to that of the present-day preacher. Murphy's readable discussion of the book helps to solve this problem by transcending a mechanical designation of speeches to this or that person in order to treat the content of their theological positions and arguments.

It is above all the "message" of the book that is Murphy's concern, and in his treatment of that message Murphy demonstrates how the Book of Job is indeed proclamation of the Word of God in response to specific questions about the meaning of life and justice and God himself.

Roland E. Murphy, O. Carm., is Professor of Old Testament at the Divinity School of Duke University. Among his numerous published books and articles are his contributions on wisdom literature, Ecclesiastes, Song of Songs, and Psalms in the *Jerome Biblical Commentary,* for which he served also as a co-editor. Professor Murphy's interest and ability in writing on biblical interpretation and proclamation is illustrated further by his membership on the Advisory Council of *Interpretation,* and on the Editorial Board of *Hermeneia:* A Historical and Critical Commentary on the Bible (Fortress Press).

Spring 1977   FOSTER R. MCCURLEY
                  Lutheran Theological Seminary at Philadelphia

PSALMS

CHAPTER ONE

INTRODUCTION

How does the Psalter fit into the *Proclamation Commentaries* series? The Psalms are liturgical prayers that reflect the whole range of human experience with God. Certain of them are more "kerygmatic" than others, especially the hymns, since they proclaim and praise the good news of the Lord's saving acts in Israel's history (e.g., Pss. 105, 114). But there are kerygmatic elements in almost all the different types of psalms. The thanksgiving psalm usually includes a witness or acknowledgment of Yahweh as savior. Even the laments utilize such themes, as in Psalm 22, "in thee our fathers trusted; they trusted, and thou didst deliver them."

However, the potential of the Psalms for preaching and speaking to the human heart is not to be measured by any narrow definition of kerygma. The fact is that they present most vividly the perennial dialogue between God and human beings. Martin Luther expressed this graphically in his preface to his 1528 translation of the Psalter:

A human heart is like a ship on a wild sea, driven by the storm winds from the four corners of the world. Here it is stuck with fear and worry about impending disaster; there comes grief and sadness because of present evil. Here breathes a breeze of hope and of anticipated happiness; there blows security and joy in present blessings. These storm winds teach us to speak with earnestness, to open the heart and pour out what lies at the bottom of it. He who is stuck in fear and need speaks of misfortune quite differently from him who floats on joy; and he who floats on joy speaks and sings of joy quite differently from him who is stuck in fear. When a sad man laughs or a glad man weeps, they say, he does not do so from the heart; that is, the depths of the heart are not open, and what is in them does not come out.

What is the greatest thing in the Psalter but this earnest speaking amid these storm winds of every kind? Where does one find finer words of joy than in the psalms of praise and thanksgiving? There you look into the hearts of all the saints, as into fair and pleasant gardens, yes, as into heaven itself. There you see what fine and pleasant flowers of the heart spring up from all sorts of fair and happy thoughts toward God, because of his blessings. On the other hand, where do you find deeper, more sorrowful, more pitiful words of sadness than in the psalms of lamentation? There again you look into the hearts of all the saints, as into death, yes, as into hell itself. How gloomy and dark it is there, with all kinds of troubled forebodings about the wrath of God! So, too, when they speak of fear and hope, they use such words that no painter could so depict for you fear or hope, and no Cicero or other orator so portray them. And that they speak these words to God and with God, this, I repeat, is the best thing of all. This gives the words double earnestness and life. For when men speak with men about these matters, what they say does not come so powerfully from the heart; it does not burn and live, is not so urgent. Hence it is that the Psalter is the book of all saints; and everyone, in whatever situation he may be, finds in that situation psalms and words that fit his case, that suit him as if they were put there just for his sake, so that he could not put it better himself, or find or wish for anything better.[1]

The high dramatic and poetic level of the Psalms is sometimes considered as a barrier to modern comprehension, as though the symbolism and imagery ("waters," "pit") strike the modern reader as too "far out." But we will argue in fact that this symbolism not only has significant value in itself, but also has preserved the Psalms from details that would limit their outreach to all peoples. In short, this imagery has enabled the Psalms to transcend inevitable cultural particularities. The preacher is not spared the task of initiating an audience into the Israelite world of thought. But once there, the audience is able to move within the universalism of this imagery. All that is needed is a certain sensitivity to poetry, a yielding to the imagery.

A noted Catholic theologian, Karl Rahner, has commented cogently and perceptively on such a need in a study entitled, "Poetry and the Christian":

And so it is true that the capacity and the practice of perceiving the poetic word is a presupposition of hearing the word of God . . . the poetic word and the poetic ear are so much part of man that if this essential power were really lost to the heart, man could no longer hear the word of God in the word of man. In its inmost essence, the poetic is a prerequisite for Christianity.[2]

The poetic is "prerequisite" in the sense that there is an innate poetic potential in all of us to react to reality by means of imagery. The biblical word actualizes this potential, and this booklet is offered as an aid in the process.

Two particularly significant insights have emerged from modern research on the Psalms. One is the fruit of form–critical studies: the recognition of the various literary types that are to be found in the Psalter, such as the hymn, thanksgiving songs, and laments. The second is the realization that these prayers are not free-floating compositions, but were composed in the first instance for liturgical worship.

The first point has made possible a fruitful approach to understanding the Psalms as literature: their setting, and their various types. The ancients were not unaware of this, in so far as in many of the pre-Christian titles to the psalms an effort was made to provide information about the setting of an individual poem. The trouble is that these notes are over-specific: "A Psalm of David, when Nathan the prophet came to him, after he had gone in to Bathsheba" (Ps. 51), or "a Miktam of David, when the Philistines seized him in Gath" (Ps. 56). We are in no position to describe the precise setting of individual psalms, or even to determine which psalms, if any, were written by David. Modern research has taught us to be more modest. We can indicate in general the setting, structure and motifs of various types of poems, and such data enable the reader to understand the psalms more honestly.

The liturgical character of the Psalter is important. If they were composed for performance in the temple, as the majority seem to have been, the use of them in Christian liturgy should be affected thereby. But the liturgical origins bear also upon the understanding of the poem itself. One must reckon, for example, with the possibility of a liturgical mime which would have accompanied Psalm 46:8, "Come, behold the works of the Lord." What are the people invited to behold? Surely some activity accompanied the poem. In the thanksgiving psalms one can see how the psalmist turns and addresses the bystanders, as in Psalm 30:4, "Sing praises to the Lord, O you his saints. . . ." Recognition of the liturgical character of these prayers provides one with a more realistic understanding of what the prayer is about.

There is no substitute for the reader's diligent application of himself or herself to an individual psalm. Reading about the Psalter is simply not as effective as studying the psalms themselves. Hence the first chapter of this book is perhaps the most important. It invites readers to make their own "confrontation" with the Psalter in the light of the literary types that have been established by modern biblical research. At times the reader will be minded to disagree with the classification of a given psalm as belonging to a certain type. In several cases there may be good reason for such disagreement, especially in those psalms which present "mixed" types. The attribution of the psalms to a given type is to be taken rather as a suggestion to the reader, which needs to be personally verified. The ensuing chapters aim at certain aspects of the theology of the Psalms which undergird both proclamation and personal appropriation.

CHAPTER TWO

LITERARY TYPES

1. *Hymn*. The hymn, or song of praise, is rather clearly structured into an introduction, body and conclusion. The introduction consists of one or several couplets in which the psalmist enthusiastically and joyously addresses himself (Ps. 104:1), or others (Pss. 33:1; 29:1; 117:1). The speaker attempts to arouse an audience to praise and acknowledgement of the Lord. Almost immediately one glides into the body of the prayer where the reasons (often introduced by "because") are given for the praise. Two reasons are most often alleged and most fully developed: God's action in creating (a continuous, sustaining action), and his saving acts in Israel's history. These two themes embrace a large range of Old Testament theology and will be considered again in later chapters. Structurally, they motivate the call to praise the Lord. The ending is simple enough; the psalmist frequently returns to the opening summons to bless or praise the Lord.

Such hymns are found throughout the Bible: the song of Miriam (Exod. 15), the song of Deborah (Judg. 5), and also in the Apocrypha (Tob. 13:2-9). The common exclamation, hallelujah ("praise Yah!" i.e., the Lord), which occurs as a title in Psalms 111—118 and in Psalms 146—150, is in itself an abbreviated hymn. Although not all may agree about the precise number of the hymns, the following psalms may be counted as such: Psalms 8, 19:1-6; 29, 33,46—48, 66:1-12; 76, 84, 87, 93, 96—100, 104, 105, 113, 117, 122, 135, 136, 145—150.

Among these hymns, a secondary classification, based on content rather than upon genre, deserves mention. The "Songs of Zion," so-called because Jerusalem or Zion is the main topic, are the following: Psalms 46, 48, 76, 84, 87, 122. The identification of the modern reader with Zion is at first sight not easy to achieve. But when one recalls the role of Jerusalem in the Old Testament, many theological ideas emerge. This was the city of David, where the temple was built, the center of the Lord's presence among his people, the place where his Name dwelt, as the Book of Deuteronomy customarily phrases it. Jerusalem signifies the Lord's presence, and its destruction in 587 B.C. is all the more poignant. Ezekiel saw the glory of the Lord departing from Jerusalem (Ezek. 9–11); mercifully, he also saw the return of the glory of the Lord (Ezek. 43:1–9). In Christian tradition and already in the New Testament, the earthly Jerusalem became the type of the heavenly Jerusalem (Gal. 4:21–31).

Another classification, guided primarily by certain liturgical references, is the enthronement psalms. Sigmund Mowinckel tied these psalms in with a particular feast of Yahweh's enthronement, celebrated on the annual feast of Tabernacles/New Year. Although Mowinckel lists over twenty enthronement psalms (8, 15, 24, 29, 33, 46, 48, 50, 66A, 75, 76, 81, 82, 84, 95, 100, 114, 118, 132, 149), the following at least can be clearly designated as dealing with the enthronement of the Lord: Psalms 47, 93, 96, 97, 98, 99. Whether or not these psalms have their original setting in a specific feast is not the issue here. The fact is that the Lord is celebrated as king in several psalms. Just as there was the cry for Jehu (2 Kings 9:13) and other kings, "N. has become king," so the same acclamation is made about the Lord (Pss. 96:10; 97:1; 99:1). Joyful celebration (Ps. 98:6) and even a procession of the ark (Ps. 47:5) seem to have formed part of the liturgy. The salutation of the Lord as king does not mean that he was not always king; his kingship is being actualized, or re–presented, in the cult. He is king because of his creative power (Pss. 93:2–4; 96:10) and because he "comes" to judge the nations (Pss. 96:13; 98:9).

2. *Psalms of Lament.* There are more laments, or complaints, than any other type in the Psalter. The lament is not a dirge or lamentation, such as is found in the Book of Lamentations or in David's lamentation over Saul and Jonathan (2 Sam. 1:19–27). The lamentation looks backward to a catastrophe; it is concerned about the death of a person, or the destruction of an area and/or its sanctuary. The lament looks forward to deliverance; it is concerned that the threatening death and destruction be eliminated, that the

psalmist or the people be delivered by the Lord. Instead of a tragic reversal (lamentation), there is a saving reversal (lament) in the psalmist's experience. The lament can be individual or national.

(a) Individual Lament. There is no agreement concerning the exact number of these psalms. Many scholars have recognized sub-categories, such as prayers of the falsely accused (Pss. 7, 35, 57, 59). The reader can note the following: Psalms 3, 5—7, 14 (=53), 17, 22, 25—28, 31, 35, 36, 38—40, 42—43, 51, 54—57, 59, 61, 64, 69—71, 86, 88, 102, 120, 130, 140—143.

The structure usually consists of the following: a) a cry for help; b) a description of the psalmist's distress, often mixed with appeals; c) reasons why the Lord should intervene; finally, d) most laments end on the note of certainty that the Lord has heard the prayer (Pss. 39 and 88 are notable exceptions), and e) the ending often includes a vow to praise God for the deliverance.

The style of the language is striking. The reader finds it impossible to pinpoint the exact nature of the distress which is being described. In Psalm 22, for example, the psalmist is surrounded by the "bulls of Bashan," dogs, even a lion, and wild oxen; there is mention of a sword, and the person is "poured out like water," the "heart is like wax." As Christoph Barth has remarked, all this could hardly happen to a person in one lifetime, much less on a single occasion. The point is that the language abounds in imagery and symbolism, without specifying the psalmist's affliction. In general one may conclude that the sufferings in the lament range from physical sickness (Ps. 38: 1–8) to spiritual disaster (sin; cf. Ps. 51). In Old Testament thought, suffering and wrongdoing are joined; there has to be a cause for the adversity one suffers—hence the agony that many experienced when they suffered for no apparent reason (Job) or when the wicked prospered (Pss. 37, 73). Paradoxically, the fact that the language of the lament does not betray the specific suffering is a gain, not a loss. By avoiding particulars and using broad symbols, this language is able to speak across centuries to all manner of afflicted people. If the psalmist had given the details of the particular affliction, later generations would have been less able to identify with the prayer. Thus, the metaphors of Psalm 69, "waters," "deep mire," "the flood" have spoken to Everyman. All have been beleaguered and bewildered at one time or another, and these symbols communicate precisely those feelings. The language of the lament deals in extremes; maximum godlessness is arrayed against all that is good in human existence. This sharp, black and white, contrast has to be weighed if one is to appropriate these prayers. Another frequent factor in the description of the distress is enemies, evildoers. These characteristics have often been a stumbling block to those who wish to use the laments in prayer—a difficulty to which we shall return later.

The description of the psalmist's distress would form a grim prayer indeed, were it not for the motifs which are adduced to move the Lord to intervene. Very often the appeal is to his *hesed* ("loving kindness," or "steadfast love"). Because of this tie which his covenant creates with his people, he is expected to intervene and save the psalmist (Ps. 6:4). Or the fact that the psalmist trusts in the Lord should induce him to hear the prayer, as in Psalm 26:1. The psalmist may even claim that personal righteousness (cf. Pss. 17 and 26) should serve as a reason for the Lord to intervene. Such statements are to be understood more as declarations of loyalty or of intent. They are not the result of a personal examination of conscience.

Perhaps the most striking feature of the lament is the ending: the certainty that the Lord has heard the prayer. This has been explained in various ways: psychological and religious certainty due to the faith of the psalmist, or the certainty belongs actually to a thanksgiving psalm uttered after the deliverance. It seems best to recognize that the transition from pleading to certainty is due to the oracle communicated by one of the temple personnel at this point in the psalm. The oracle has not been preserved in the lament itself, but there are suggestions of such oracles in other psalms. For example, a priest would have responded to the prayer with words like, "do not fear" or "the Lord is your salvation." There are hints of such moments in the psalms (12:6; 35:3; 85:8; 91:14–15; 121:3–5), but there is no explicit description in the Psalter of the giving of such an oracle.

(b) The Lament of the Nation. In contrast to the individual lament, this is a complaint of the community, and it would have marked special days of fasting or mourning, especially after a military reversal, a drought, or other disaster. A day of national penance would be proclaimed, and appropriate rites re-enacted at the temple. Among these prayers may be counted Psalms 44, 60, 74, 79, 80, 83, 85, 89, 90, 94:1–7, 123. The structure is similar to the individual lament: a) an appeal for help; b) a description of distress (usually consisting in a reproach—how long?—directed against God, a statement of national affliction, and a reference to the role of the oppressor); c) an expression of trust, and often d) a vow to offer thanksgiving.

Looking back over the structure of the lament, we see that it travels a path from brokenness to wholeness, from complaint to praise. Both Claus Westermann and Walter Brueggemann have emphasized this aspect.[3] The lament is usually turned into praise. In these psalms suffering gives way to joy. The very structure of Israel's salvation history sets this pattern. Thus we find the pattern in the canticle of Hezekiah (2 Kings 20:3–7) or in the "little credo" of Deuteronomy 26:5–9. Israel is afflicted; she calls to the Lord for help; the Lord hears:

> A wandering Aramean was my father; and he went down into Egypt and sojourned there, few in number; and there he became a nation . . . And the Egyptians treated us harshly . . . Then we cried to the Lord the God of our fathers, and the Lord heard our voice, and saw our affliction . . . and the Lord brought us out of Egypt . . . (Deut. 26:5–9).

The cry of distress goes with the deliverance that is expected. The appeal to God's compassion—which is an accurate description of the function of the lament—is to be answered by the Lord who is concerned for his people. As Brueggemann has put it, "Israel's history is shaped and interpreted as an experience of cry and rescue."[4]

3. *Psalms of Trust.* The motif of trust, as a reason for the Lord to intervene, was already noted as a frequent characteristic of the psalms of lament. This motif can also constitute an entire prayer, as in the following Psalms: 4, 11, 16, 23, 27:1–6; 62:1–8; 125, 131.

4. *Royal Psalms.* This designation flows from content, not structure; the king is at the center of the prayer. There are several genres included: Psalm 18 is a royal psalm of thanksgiving uttered by a king; Psalm 20 (and 144:1–11) is a plea for the king's safety; Psalm 21 is a thanksgiving for the divine blessing accorded to the king; Psalm 45 hails the king on the occasion of his marriage; Psalms 2, 72, 110 are best understood as referring to the king's accession to the throne (or the anniversary).

Because Mowinckel was particularly struck by what he conceived as the role of the king in temple worship, he was able to speak of several more poems as "royal psalms." In certain psalms there is an alternation of "I" and "we," that points to the role of a cultic leader. The king would be the representative of the community, thus a "corporate personality." In the course of time these royal/congregational psalms would have come to be "democratized" for the use of the laity. Among these Mowinckel would number Psalms 18, 28, 61, 63, etc. (for further discussion, see *The Psalms in Israel's Worship I*, 106–192).

In a narrower, but more explicit sense, the royal psalms can be enumerated: Psalms 2, 18, 20, 21, 45, 72, 101, 110. The themes commemorated here are rooted in the *magna carta* of Old Testament (royal) messianism (the term, messiah, properly means "the anointed," i.e., the king): the oracle of Nathan to David, related in 2 Samuel 7. The promise of an eternal dynasty became the basis for the messianic development in prophets such as Isaiah (the "book of Immanuel" in Isa. 7—11), Micah and others. The themes of (adoptive) sonship, world-wide rule, justice, and peace appear in the royal psalms. They are not to be put down as merely exaggerated court style, the flattery and terminology characteristic of the rulers of the ancient Near East. The similarities between these themes and the praise of the rulers of Egypt and Mesopotamia are undeniable. But in Israel's case, the promise of the Lord of heaven and earth was understood to stand behind the Davidic ruler. The Psalms refer directly to a reigning Jerusalem monarch, but they envision him in the light of the promise to David. He was the vehicle of blessing, and thus of the messianic hope for his people. The agony caused by the apparent destruction of this hope in 587 B.C. is obvious from Psalm 89. Readers would do well to ponder the fact that these royal psalms were handed down and preserved in the centuries that followed the catastrophe of 587 B.C. when there was no longer a son of David reigning in Jerusalem. The point is that these psalms were reinterpreted in a more eschatological and personal messianic sense, as the so-called "Psalms of Solomon" of the first century B.C. suggest (Pss. 17 and 18).

5. *Wisdom Psalms.* There is considerable difference of opinion whether this is a viable classification. Yet several scholars use the phrase, even if they do not agree as to the number of psalms which

it includes. The reader will be challenged by a consideration of the following: Psalms 1, 32, 34, 37, 49, 111, 112. Some would include Psalm 119, although this is perhaps better considered as *sui generis,* a Torah or "Law" psalm. Again, Psalm 73 is frequently considered to be a wisdom poem because it deals with retribution, but the presence of this one theme is hardly enough to determine the character of the poem. One should look for the following characteristics in weighing the classification of wisdom psalms: a) the contrast between the just and the wicked; b) advice concerning conduct; c) fear of the Lord; d) the presence of comparisons and admonitions; e) alphabetic (acrostic) sequence of verses; f) "better" sayings; g) the address to a "son"; h) the "blessed" (*'ašrê*) formula. These are characteristic features of Old Testament wisdom literature, and hence they provide some criteria for judgment.

6. *Liturgies.* In the broad sense, this classification might include most of the Psalter because the psalms have their specific origins, as we have seen, in the temple liturgy. However, the term can be more conveniently used of certain psalms in which the structure is actually formed by solo and choral recitation. Under this rubric will be gathered several types of liturgies which most scholars distinguish one from another.

(a) Entrance Liturgies. These are striking examples of the liturgical genre: Psalms 15 and 24:3–6. Imitations of this type are to be found in Isaiah 33:14–16, Micah 6:6–8, and Ezekiel 18:5–17. The liturgy is composed of two basic elements: (1) the request to enter the temple, uttered by the faithful, either individually or in a group (Pss. 15:1; 24:3); (2) the response, presumably uttered by a priest, which lists the demands that must be fulfilled before one can present one's self to the Lord (Pss. 15:2–6; 24:4–6). Usually the liturgy ends with a formula which states apodictically that the just person has a right to enter the temple (Pss. 15:5; 24:6). The moral qualities required for entrance are derived from the decalogue (Pss. 15:3–5; 24:4), and a special rite at the temple gate is described in Psalm 24:7–16 (cf. Isa. 26:1).

(b) Oracles of Divine Protection. Although Psalms 91 and 121 are classified in various ways by scholars, they seem to fit better here. In Psalm 121 the worshiper pronounces the first two verses, and then receives the promise of divine protection, communicated in an oracle from a priest, in verses 3–8. Psalm 91 in its entirety is parallel to Psalm 121:3–8 in that it also constitutes a priestly oracle of assurance; the words of the worshiper are quoted in verse 2, and the oracle of the Lord is directly given in the final verses, 14–16.

(c) Liturgy of Divine Judgment. These poems deal with Israel's breaking of the covenant: Psalms 50, 81, 95 and perhaps 78. The indictment is made directly by the Lord himself (through one of the temple personnel): "Hear!" (Pss. 50:7; 81:8; cf. 95:7). In Psalm 78 the psalmist addresses the people, in a didactic manner (v. 2; cf. Ps. 49:1–4), and describes Israel's history as one of disobedience and ingratitude; this poem is often grouped with the so-called "historical psalms" (Pss. 105, 106, 135, 136).

This discussion of the literary types within the Psalter is basic to understanding and utilizing the Psalms. Although there is a wide range of consensus among scholars concerning the classification of the psalms, there are also differences of opinion. This is not as disadvantageous as it might seem to be at first sight. Rather, it is a challenge to the reader to enter into a psalm, and to weigh the evidence that suggests that it belongs to a specific genre. In this way the psalm is appropriated and personalized. In short, there is no escape from an encounter, even a confrontation, with a psalm, and the approach by way of literary types is too profitable to be neglected. On such a solid basis one can build a theology of the Psalter, and evaluate the potential of the Psalms for proclamation. The succeeding chapters are an attempt in that direction.

CHAPTER THREE

THEOLOGICAL THEMES

The Psalms are a rich source of theology. In recent times two views of Old Testament theology have emerged. Gerhard von Rad understands it as dealing with Israel's explicit assertions or testimonies about Yahweh, for example, the "credo" of Deuteronomy 26:5–9. W. Eichrodt sees it as a complete portrayal of Israel's realm of belief, especially in view of covenant. In either view, the Psalter stands up well as a reflection of Israel's belief. Artur Weiser, in his commentary on Psalms, is somewhat extreme when he interprets the psalms largely in the context of covenant renewal. The psalms are not to be limited to any particular event. They form a cross-section of the prayer–life and temple worship of the Israelites over several centuries, and into them has been incorporated almost every aspect of Israel's world view and belief. In this case, as in so many others, the old saying *lex orandi, lex credendi* (law of prayer is law of belief) proves eminently true.

LITURGY

The liturgical worship of Israel was vivid and demonstrative. It was seen as "service" (*ᵃbōdāh*), and the true worshiper was a "servant" (*'ebed*). The rites were carried out in the temple, which was the religious center of the people, the place where dwelt the Lord's "Name" (Deut. 12:5; 1 Kings 8:29). Although the building itself was of modest proportions, it was located in an inner court that was in turn framed by a large courtyard or outer court, several hundred yards in extent. When one recalls the bronze altar of sacrifices, the altar of incense, the table of shewbread and ten candlesticks, and the "sea of bronze," it is easy to imagine the colorful pageantry that must have marked the various rites. There were no images of the

Lord, but songs and processions in his honor abounded (Hallelu-Yah!). The writer of Psalm 42 could reminisce:

> These things I remember,
>   as I pour out my soul:
> how I went with the throng,
>   and led them in procession to the house of God,
> with glad shouts and songs of thanksgiving,
>   a multitude keeping festival (Ps. 42:4).

Perhaps the most vivid descriptions of liturgical celebration are Psalms 47 and 95:

> Clap your hands, all peoples!
>   Shout to God with loud songs of joy! . . .
> God has gone up with a shout,
>   the Lord with the sound of a trumpet.
> Sing praises to God, sing praises!
>   Sing praises to our King, sing praises! (Ps. 47:1, 5–6).

Directions are given to the congregation, and a procession seems to be described (v. 5). Most probably the ark of the covenant (upon which the Lord was invisibly enthroned) was carried in procession (47:8, "God sits on his holy throne"). The exhortation to the worshiping community is given in Psalm 95:

> O come, let us sing to the Lord;
>   let us make a joyful noise to the rock of our salvation!
> Let us come into his presence with thanksgiving;
>   let us make a joyful noise to him with
>   songs of praise! . . .
> O come, let us worship and bow down,
>   let us kneel before the Lord, our Maker!
> For he is our God,
>   and we are the people of his pasture,
>   and the sheep of his hand (Ps. 95:1–2, 6–7).

In this psalm the speech of the Lord should be noted:

> O that today you would hearken to his voice!
>   Harden not your hearts . . .
> For forty years I loathed that generation . . . (Ps. 95:7–10).

This is a divine oracle which was uttered by one of the temple personnel: an appeal to heed the Lord, warning against the disobedience that characterized the past. Several oracles appear in the psalms, thus reflecting the liturgical ceremonies of which they formed a part (Pss. 46:10; 50). Other psalms contain references to an action that seems to be taking place: "Come and see what God has done" (Ps. 66:5); "Walk about Zion, go round about her, number her towers" (Ps. 48:12).

The structure of certain psalms clearly indicates that they are liturgies. Choral recitation is obvious from the refrain in Psalm 136 (cf. Ps. 118:2–4), "for his steadfast love endures for ever." The change of person in Psalm 121:3–7 (cf. Ps. 134:3) indicates that one of the temple functionaries, most likely a priest, imparts a blessing. There was also the so-called "torah-liturgy," which took place at the gate of the temple (Pss. 15, 24). In question and answer form, the worshiper recognizes the qualities requisite for one who enters the temple to serve the Lord:

> O Lord, who shall sojourn in thy tent?
>> Who shall dwell on thy holy hill?
> He who walks blamelessly, and does what is right,
>> and speaks truth from his heart;
> who does not slander with his tongue,
>> and does no evil to his friend,
>> nor takes up a reproach against his neighbor;
> in whose eyes a reprobate is despised,
>> but who honors those who fear the Lord;
> who swears to his own hurt and does not change;
>> who does not put out his money at interest,
>> and does not take a bribe against the innocent.
> He who does these things shall never be moved (Ps. 15).

The torah-liturgy does not allow the worshiper to rest in complacency. It is rather a recognition of the fact that one who approaches the Lord may not do so in a casual manner; an effort to abide by his will must be made. The ideals mentioned here bear upon one's relationship to others (slander, reproach, bribery). The declaration is in the direction of the New Testament injunction (Matt. 5:23–24) to be reconciled with one's neighbor before offering sacrifice: What requirements are demanded of those who worship the Lord?

Closely related to this are the statements of personal integrity which occur frequently in the psalms. The motif of innocence has a prominent role in Psalm 17, which begins with placing a "just cause" before the Lord:

> If thou triest my heart, if thou visitest me by night,
>> if thou testest me, thou wilt find no wickedness in me;
>> my mouth does not transgress.
> With regard to the works of men, by the word of thy lips
>> I have avoided the ways of the violent.
> My steps have held fast to thy paths,
>> my feet have not slipped (Ps. 17:3–5).

The protestation of innocence is actually a reason designed to move the Lord to intervene in favor of the psalmist:

> Vindicate me, O Lord,
>> for I have walked in my integrity,
>> and I have trusted in the Lord without wavering. . . .
> I wash my hands in innocence,
>> and go about thy altar, O Lord,
> singing aloud a song of thanksgiving,
>> and telling all thy wondrous deeds (Ps. 26:1, 6–7).

These expressions are not to be read in the context of the biblical parable of the Pharisee and the publican (Luke 18:10–14). They are not proud and invidious comparisons with others. They simply state where the psalmist is. They are not so much an examination of conscience as a declaration of loyalty before the Lord, and hence a reason for him to come to the defense of his servant.

SALVATION HISTORY AND CREATION

These two themes are common in the Torah, the prophets, and in the Psalms. The classical period of salvation history was the total exodus experience, leading into the possession of the Promised Land. At first reading, the commemoration of the Lord's saving deeds might seem to be only a matter of ancient history, a kind of antiquarianism particularly difficult for moderns to be attracted to. But there is more than mere memory at work here; there is "re–presentation," a biblical manner of reaching into the past and re–living it. This is illustrated in the speech of Moses in Deuteronomy 5:1–3. Moses is speaking to those who were second–generation Israelites; they had *not* been present at Sinai/Horeb. To them he nevertheless says, "Hear, O Israel . . . The Lord our God made a covenant with us in Horeb. Not with our fathers did the Lord make this covenant, but with us, who are all of us here alive this day." The contradiction is startling, and it is to be explained by this attitude of re–presenting the covenant. The great events of the past are recalled and celebrated as if they are present. The liturgy offered an opportunity for just that kind of celebration:

> When Israel went forth from Egypt,
> > the house of Jacob from a people of strange language, . . .
> The sea looked and fled,
> > Jordan turned back.
> The mountains skipped like rams,
> > the hills like lambs.
> What ails you, O sea, that you flee?
> > O Jordan, that you turn back? (Ps. 114:1, 3–5).

The saving events of the past are being re–lived in the liturgical present. This biblical understanding of the union of past and present is persistent in the history of God's people, and it is continued in the New Testament liturgy of the "breaking of the bread": "Do this in remembrance of me . . . For as often as you eat this bread and drink the cup, you proclaim the Lord's death until he comes" (1 Cor. 11:24–26).

Psalms 105 and 106, although back–to–back in the Psalter, are an interesting contrast in the rehearsal of Israel's salvation history. Psalm 105 is a straight presentation of God's wondrous deeds: the covenant with the patriarchs, the story of Joseph, the exodus and the marvels in the desert, and the possession of the land. Israel is summoned to sing these praises, to make them known among the peoples, to "remember the wonderful works he has done" (v. 5). But in Psalm 106 the sacred history is used not for praise, but as an expression of sorrow. The disobedient and faithless conduct of Israel is highlighted: not recognizing the Lord's works when they were in Egypt, rebelling at the Red Sea, craving for the quail, the revolt of Dathan and Abiram, murmuring in the desert, the apostasy to the Baal of Peor, and the incident at Meribah. In its present form the poem is a liturgy of lament of a people in exile (v. 47), a proclamation of sinfulness (v. 6). While it is not a lament, Psalm 78 shows some similarity to Psalm 106, in that the salvation history is used for a specific purpose. On this occasion, it is to teach. History is used as a lesson: the emphasis on Israel's rebelliousness is indicated in the refrains (vv. 17, 32, 40, 56). In contrast to the other psalms which survey salvation history (Pss. 105, 136), this one includes the choice of David and of Zion as the culminating events of the Lord's saving action.

The development of creation theology in the Old Testament is extensive. The priestly tradition (Gen. 1) uses the majestic sequence of six days to portray the effortless achievement of God's word ("And God said. . . ." cf. Pss. 33:6; 148:5). The Yahwist narrative pictures the Lord creating as a potter working with clay on the wheel (Gen. 2:7, "then the Lord God formed. . . ."). In the poetic narratives of Isaiah, Job and Psalms, a different approach is used. God has to overcome chaos, which is personified as Rahab or Leviathan (Isa. 51:9–10; Pss. 89:10; 74:14). These bold imaginative descriptions are among the best poetry of the Bible:

> O Lord, how manifold are thy works!
>   In wisdom hast thou made them all;
>   the earth is full of thy creatures.
> Yonder is the sea, great and wide,
>   which teems with things innumerable,
>   living things both small and great.
> There go the ships,
>   and Leviathan which thou didst form
>   to sport in it (Ps. 104:24–26).

This is not the place to elaborate on the mythical background of the biblical presentation of creation. The Enuma Elish epic of Mesopotamia and the myths of Ugarit were the seedbed of Israel's views. The peoples of the ancient Near East all knew of a creator God. What is distinctive of Israel is the way in which the doctrine of creation was co–ordinated with Israel's saving experience. Gerhard von Rad was the first to develop this idea (*Old Testament Theology,* I,

136–139). Actually, he spoke of the subordination of creation to salvation history because Yahwism regarded itself "exclusively" as a religion of salvation. While one may demur at this narrow definition of Yahwism, there is no denying that Israel correlated creation and salvation. Deutero–Isaiah could speak of "the Lord, he who created you, O Jacob, he who formed you, O Israel" (Isa. 43:1; cf. 45:9–12).

Psalm 89 begins by celebrating the "gracious deeds" (RSV, "steadfast love," v. 1) of the Lord, and it concentrates on the covenant with David (only to end up with the lament that the Lord has broken his covenant). But included in these acts of God is creation:

> Thou dost rule the raging of the sea;
>> when its waves rise, thou stillest them.
> Thou didst crush Rahab like a carcass,
>> thou didst scatter thy enemies with
>>> thy mighty arm (Ps. 89:9–10).

Psalm 74 is another poem that associates creation with salvation:

> Yet God my King is from of old,
>> working salvation in the midst of the earth.
> Thou didst divide the sea by thy might;
>> thou didst break the heads of the dragons on the waters.
> Thou didst crush the heads of Leviathan,
>> thou didst give him as food
>>> for the creatures of the wilderness (Ps. 74:12–14).

More literally, the word for salvation in verse 12 is in the plural, "saving acts," and it is explained by the following verses which interweave the crossing of the Red Sea with the slaying of the powers of chaos in creation. The imagery for creation and salvation is interchangeable.

In view of this association of salvation and creation, it is not surprising that the creation narrative in the book of Genesis (chaps. 1ff.) is prefixed to the beginning of salvation history (Gen. 12:1–3, the Lord's commission to Abraham). Creation is a work of the Lord at the beginning of history, and not a mythic reality, even if it is described in terms drawn from myth.

It should not be thought that creation is merely an appendage to salvation history. It is relished in and for itself, as many psalms prove. In particular, it is seen as a continuous act on the part of the Lord. His victory over the powers of chaos is not instantaneous; it is an ongoing battle. If he did not keep chaos in check, creation could be undone. Psalm 104 fills out the details:

> Thou makest springs gush forth in the valleys;
>   they flow between the hills,
> they give drink to every beast of the field;
>   the wild asses quench their thirst.
> By them the birds of the air have their habitation;
>   they sing among the branches. . . .
> Thou dost cause the grass to grow for the cattle,
>   and plants for man to cultivate,
> that he may bring forth food from the earth,
>   and wine to gladden the heart of man (Ps. 104:10–15).

There is a real feeling for the living things, the material things: wine, oil, animals, meadows, pastures, grain. A beautiful harvest is described in Psalm 65:

> Thou visitest the earth and waterest it,
>   thou greatly enrichest it;
> the river of God is full of water;
>   thou providest their grain,
>   for so thou hast prepared it.
> Thou waterest its furrows abundantly
>   settling its ridges,
> softening it with showers,
>   and blessing its growth.
> Thou crownest the year with thy bounty;
>   the tracks of thy chariot drip with fatness . . .
> the meadows clothe themselves with flocks,
>   the valleys deck themselves with grain,
>   they shout and sing together for joy (Ps. 65:9–13).

The enumeration of the good things of this world reminds us how "earthy" the Old Testament is. It does not spiritualize the realities of life; it accepts them in all their materiality as gifts, blessings. Such is a sacramental view of the universe. The world spoke to Israel of its creator:

The heavens are telling the glory of God;
   and the firmament proclaims his handiwork.
Day to day pours forth speech,
   and night to night declares knowledge (Ps. 19:1–2).

THE ANOINTED

Contrary to popular opinion, it is the king and not the priest who is truly anointed, or as the Hebrew term has it, the "messiah." Anointing came to be applied eventually to the priest, but originally it was reserved for the king as a sacred person. The depth of feeling that the term connoted is shown in David's reaction to a suggestion that he should rid himself of Saul when he had him in a vulnerable position (1 Sam. 24:1–7; 26:6–10): "The Lord forbid that I should do this thing to my lord, the Lord's anointed, to put forth my hand against him, seeing he is the Lord's anointed."

The central role of the king in the life of the nation is almost beyond our comprehension. Mowinckel described royal ideology of the ancient Near East in the following terms: "The king is thus the representative of the gods on earth, the steward of the god or the gods. Through him they exercise their power and sovereignty, and he is the channel through which blessing and happiness and fertility flow from the gods to men . . .

"But he is also man's representative before the gods. In him the people is one. According to the corporate view of those times the people was somehow incorporated in him, and the strength and blessing which he receives from the gods were partaken of by the whole country and the people.

"This double position of the king as the link between gods and men is expressed and made effective through the cult. He is the high priest. . . ."[5] Mowinckel allows that the Yahwistic religion altered fundamentally this broad royal ideology (one thinks of the boldness of the prophetic opposition to the anointed kings!). Nevertheless, there is a real influence of the ancient Near Eastern ideology upon the position of the anointed in Israel, and the language which expresses his person and achievements. He, too, bears a special relationship to the Lord. He has the Lord's spirit; he was chosen by the Lord and adopted as son. He is, in short, "the breath of life" (Lam. 4:20) of the people. We shall see that the dynastic oracle of 2 Samuel 7 has played a role in the Israelite concept of the anointed.

It is understandable then that one of the leading figures in the temple liturgy was the king, and several psalms reflect his role. His accession to the throne, or the anniversary of this event, is celebrated in Psalms 2, 72, and 110. The marriage of an Israelite king to a foreign princess is the background of Psalm 45. Psalms 18 and 21 are a royal thanksgiving for victory in war. There are pleas for the king's safety and victory in Psalms 20 and 144:1–11 (these verses probably spoken by the king). It is not surprising that Mowinckel went so far as to speak of a "democratization" of several psalms (e.g., 44, 66, 144). That is to say, in the course of time, several royal psalms were seen as applicable to every person, and so they entered into the common liturgical prayers of the temple.

The royal psalms seem exaggerated to us. They refer to the reigning king in terminology that is reminiscent of the court style of the powerful monarchs of the ancient Near East. Thus his rule can be described as "from sea to sea, and from the River [Euphrates] to the ends of the earth" (Ps. 72:8; cf. 2:8).To world-wide empire corresponds eternal rule, with peace and justice (Ps. 72:1–7). He is even called an "elohim" being (Ps. 45:6, RSV margin), for he is begotten of God (Ps. 2:7). All these prerogatives follow from the fact that the Lord stands behind him. It is the Lord who installs him (Ps. 2)and supports him against his enemies (Ps. 110).

One might well put this in the same category of the florid court style of Mesopotamia and Egypt, were it not for the oracle of Nathan to David (2 Sam. 7). This divine promise assured David that his dynasty would ever rule on in Jerusalem, and it is to be viewed as the *magna carta* or keystone of royal messianism in the Old Testament. From it stems the extensive "messianic" statements of the prophets, notably Isaiah, Micah and Jeremiah. Isaiah had his problems with the Davidic dynasty in the person of king Ahaz, but nonetheless he envisioned a renewal of the Davidic dynasty, and he describes the ideal king in the so-called book of Immanuel (Isa. 7—11) and the righteous rule of the king is presented in chapter 32. Chapters 4 and 5 of Micah are in the same vein. The "branch" or "shoot" of Jeremiah 23:5 (=33:15) becomes a title for a new Davidic leader. References to the restoration of the Davidic house are also found in Amos 9:11 and Hosea 3:5. The hope in the Davidic dynasty is reflected particularly in Psalms 89 and 132.

Psalm 132 is a sheer celebration of the promise to David. With some exaggeration his solicitude for the Lord and the future temple is described as an oath (Ps. 132:1–5). To this corresponds the Lord's oath (no longer a promise!) about the sons of David forever sitting upon his throne (Ps. 132:11, 12, 17). The agony which the promise generated is described in Psalm 89. First the royal prerogatives are described: anointing (v. 20), divine protection (v. 21), adoptive sonship (vv. 26–27), the security of the dynasty (vv. 29–32). The Lord is described as saying: "I will not violate my covenant" (v. 34). Then the lament of the psalmist begins (vv. 38ff.). The Lord is accused of having renounced his covenant, in view of the humiliation suffered by the king, and a plea is entered for restoration.

How are these royal psalms to be judged from a theological point of view? The exegetical tradition of the past, especially in the church fathers, understood them as predictions of Jesus Christ, the messiah. Obviously, they refer in the literal historical sense to the currently reigning king, or a Davidic descendant that is on the historical horizon, but not to an eschatological figure of the end-time. Hence one might say that the old exegetical tradition telescopes, or over–simplifies the royal messianism of the Psalter. But this should not prevent us from appreciating the importance of royal messianism. This was a magnificent vision of the reigning king, a hope placed in him as a member of a fated dynasty. He was considered to be the vehicle of God's plans for Israel, for the Lord's word to his servant David could not be allowed to fall short of fulfillment. Hence these psalms were preserved, despite the failure of kingship, despite the fact that the Davidic dynasty came to the humiliating end with the fall of Jerusalem in 587 B.C. They were reinterpreted, and in the restoration period the hope in Davidic messianism springs up anew around Zerubbabel (see the vision of Haggai and Zechariah). But almost as quickly it disappears. Royal messianism is, however, a hardy belief. The apocryphal "Psalms of Solomon" of the first century B.C. testify to beliefs in a royal Davidic figure who will lead Israel. The infancy narratives of the New Testament are influenced by royal messianism, but it is ironic that Jesus himself plays down the theme (e.g., Mark 8:29–30).

WISDOM AND TORAH

The introductory chapter listed certain psalms that seem to be related to the wisdom literature (on Old Testament wisdom see below in the introduction to Job). There is little agreement concerning which psalms should be so classified. Perhaps the case is stated better by speaking of wisdom influence upon the psalms. Rather than being a particular classification, wisdom psalms designate those various genres (hymn, thanksgiving, etc.) which have been shaped by wisdom influence, and incorporate typical wisdom teaching.

At first sight there might seem to be a contradiction between temple and school, between liturgy and wisdom, between liturgical songs of praise and wisdom pieces that inculcate lessons. However, the liturgy itself offers an occasion for teaching. In particular, the thanksgiving psalms provide for a "witness" to be given by the one who has been delivered from distress. Thus, in Psalm 30 there is unmistakable teaching in the words to the bystanders:

> For his anger is but for a moment,
>   and his favor is for a lifetime.
> Weeping may tarry for the night,
>   but joy comes with the morning (Ps. 30:5).

Since the psalmist acknowledges the Lord as a deliverer, it is also true that "what happened to me can happen to you." And so this teaching is proclaimed.

Although Psalm 34 is in appearance a song of thanksgiving, there is noticeable wisdom influence present. After the acknowledgment of the Lord's rescue ("I sought the Lord, and he answered me, and delivered me from all my fears," v. 4), the psalmist becomes teacher:

> The angel of the Lord encamps
>   around those who fear him, and delivers them.
> O taste and see that the Lord is good!
>   Happy is the man who takes refuge in him!
> O fear the Lord, you his saints,
>   for those who fear him have no want! (Ps. 34:7–9)

There is a place for wisdom teaching in the very structure of the liturgy, as the psalms of thanksgiving attest.

The Scandinavian scholar, Sigmund Mowinckel, spoke of wisdom psalms as "learned psalmography." Because he set liturgy and wisdom in such opposing categories, he was unwilling to recognize the role of such psalms in temple worship. But the fact is that we are quite ignorant of the liturgy of the second temple. The Chronicler reflects how some psalms were used in the liturgy of his day (1 Chron. 16:7–36; 29:10–13), but we are without enough evidence to say if wisdom psalms were used in the liturgy of the second temple.

There are two very explicit wisdom psalms which appear to be simple teaching, without a hint of liturgy, Psalms 37 and 49. Psalm 37 presents straightforwardly the traditional wisdom doctrine on retribution, and thus forms a counterpart to Job's three friends. It consists of admonitions and sayings which drive home the idea that the wicked will perish and the just will prosper. Therefore the just are not to envy the prosperity of the wicked. Their success can be only ephemeral, and eventually they will receive their due reward. In the meantime, one is to trust in the Lord.

Psalm 49 seems to break new paths. It begins on a solemn note, addressed to all peoples and proclaiming a message of *ḥokmāh* ("wisdom"; v. 3; with parallel terms of understanding, proverb and riddle in vv. 3–4). The issue, as in Psalm 37, is that of divine retribution. The psalmist derives some consolation from the fact that "you can't take it with you," and "no man can ransom himself" (v. 7) from death. This is an instance of human similarity to beasts (vv. 12, 20, a refrain; cf. Eccles. 3:18–21). The psalmist underscores the fate of the wicked: Death shall shepherd them in Sheol (v. 14; a doubtful Hebrew reading has, "the upright shall have dominion over them"). The RSV prefers to emend this doubtful verse, but there is no mistaking the thrust of the following verse 15: "But God will ransom my soul from the power of Sheol, for he will receive me." This stands in vivid contrast to verse 7, where it was stated that no man can redeem himself from death. Is this ransom one that only God can achieve, the ransom from mortality? Many commentators think so, and they point to the fact that God will "receive" the psalmist as he also "took" (the same verb in Hebrew, *lqḥ*) Enoch who walked before him (Gen. 5:24). Such an interpretation would be a clear intimation of immortality with God. The "wisdom" proclaimed at the outset of the poem is then centered on the blessed immortality that awaits the wise, in contrast to the ephemeral existence of the wicked.

The same contrast between the fate of the wicked and that of the just appears also in Psalm 73. The description of the "end" (v. 17) of the wicked adopts the language that is typical for the wicked: "fall to ruin," "destroyed," "swept away." But the language reserved for the just (vv. 23–28) is affirmative and very personal: "continually with thee," "receive me into glory," "my portion for ever." Here, too, there seems to be a glimpse beyond death into a union of the psalmist with God. This is not because the words, "continually," "for ever," occur; these terms in Hebrew merely indicate indefinite duration, not eternity. Similarly, "heaven" in verse 25, is the physical space above the firmament, and parallel to "earth" in verse 25b; it is not the heaven of blessed immortality. However, the "I-thou" character of the passage is striking; the key to immortality seems to be union with God, achieved in this life and enduring beyond death. There is no speculation concerning the "how," whether by reason of the nature of the soul (which is not a biblical category) or by reason of the resurrection of the body. The discussion of the problem of retribution is hardly sufficient reason to qualify Psalm 73 as a wisdom poem, but its description of the intimate relationship between God and his servant remains unsurpassed.

Hebrew wisdom was initially anchored in daily experience, where questions of good and bad were judged. It was "good" for a person to be honest (Prov. 11:4; 12:22) and diligent (Prov. 10:4, 18:9), because such conduct was self-rewarding. It was when these practical rules of life were confronted with contradiction that doubts arose, as shown in Psalm 73:1–2, and in the books of Job and Ecclesiastes. In all this the notion of wisdom is expanded beyond mere experience. It came to be seen as a gift of God, and even personified as a mystery originating from God before the creative act (Job 28; Prov. 8), and still promising life to her followers (Prov. 8:35). In the post–exilic period Israel turned to the Torah, or Law, with remarkable attention and devotion, and Law and wisdom were identified. Moses is described as addressing Israel in Deuteronomy 4:6, "Keep them [statutes and ordinances] and do them; for that will be your wisdom and your understanding in the sight of the peoples, who, when they hear all these statutes, will say, 'Surely this great nation is a wise and understanding people.' " Ben Sira, or Sirach, who wrote at the beginning of the second century B.C., presents the most striking interpretation of personified wisdom. She is personified as ruling over every people; she sought a resting place among them, but the Creator ordered her to take up her dwelling in Israel (Ecclus. 24:1–8). Then she "took root in an honored people, in the portion of the Lord, who is their inheritance" (v. 9). Sirach explicitly identifies her with the Torah: "the book of the covenant of the Most High God, the law which Moses commanded us, as an inheritance for the congregation of Jacob" (v. 22).

It is important to approach this emphasis on Torah/wisdom in an open manner and without any preconceptions about legalism. Israel viewed the Torah or Pentateuch, as the highest embodiment of the will of God, and several psalms give us a glimpse of a "torah piety." Psalm 19 can describe the Law thus:

> The Law of the Lord is perfect,
>   reviving the soul;
> The testimony of the Lord is sure,
>   making wise the simple;
> the precepts of the Lord are right,
>   rejoicing the heart;
> the commandment of the Lord is pure,
>   enlightening the eyes. . . .
> More to be desired are they than gold. . . . (Ps. 19:7–10).

This particular psalm is interesting because it is composite. What is drawn together is, appropriately, creation and Law. In view of the fact that wisdom theology is creation theology, that is, it works within the framework of the doctrine of creation, there is an inner logic that binds the two pieces (vv. 1–6; 7–14) together.

Far from being a burden, the Law is a source of joy to the true Israelite, as Psalm 1:2 testifies about the blessedness of the man whose "delight is in the law of the Lord," upon which "he meditates day and night." It is tempting to see Psalm 1 as a Torah psalm which has been deliberately placed at the opening of the Psalter to suggest to the reader the revelation of God and his will that awaits him in these poems. The longest poem in the Psalter is Psalm 119, and it is given over entirely to a meditation upon the Law. It is composed in acrostic fashion. That is to say, each successive stanza of eight lines begins with successive letters of the Hebrew alphabet, *aleph, beth,* etc. Moreover, each verse contains the word "law" or a synonym (word, statutes, commandments, precepts, ordinances, testimonies). Again, the emphasis is on the life and joy which the Law communicates to the faithful Israelite (Ps. 119:14, 40, 77, 97, 105, 127, 156, 165, 174).

SUFFERING, DEATH AND VIOLENCE

It is not easy for us to enter into and to identify with the sufferings of another. We find it difficult to shed our own concerns, and the troubles of others tend to be remote. The details of a particular distress tend to remain too particular, too individual, to speak to the community. One's personal tale of woe seldom triggers the same reaction in another. While a person may sympathize with another, he can hardly identify with the other. Yet this is what the laments of the Psalter ask of those who use them in prayer: a certain identification with the distress of the psalmist.

There is a curious paradox here. When one takes pains to identify exactly what the psalmist is complaining about, no sure answer emerges. Only in the most general way can one say that the cause of the lament is sickness (Pss. 38:3–5; 41:3,8) or unjust oppression (Pss. 7, 17, 35) or personal sin (clearly in Ps. 51). Last, but not least, there are the psalmist's enemies, who have been variously but uncertainly identified as sorcerers, class oppressors, or political foes. The fact is that the specifics of the complaint elude us, and the paradox is that this is a gain for those who wish to appropriate the lament to their own use. For if the description of the distress were quite specific, the effect would be lost on us. We are all aware of the banalities that people often complain about: a backache, the last operation, a migraine. If we have suffering in our own lives, we are not going to identify with the details of another's troubles—unless they are general enough to express our own needs. The language of the psalms has precisely this broad appeal for all who suffer; the symbolism is universal. No one has difficulty in empathizing with the following descriptions:

> Deep calls to deep
>   at the thunder of thy cataracts;
> all thy waves and thy billows
>   have gone over me (Ps. 42:7).

> Save me, O God!
>   For the waters have come up to my neck.

I sink in deep mire,
   where there is no foothold;
I have come into deep waters,
   and the flood sweeps over me (Ps. 69:1–2).

For my soul is full of troubles,
   and my life draws near to Sheol.
I am reckoned among those who go down to the Pit;
   I am a man who has no strength,
like one forsaken among the dead,
   like the slain that lie in the grave,
like those whom thou dost remember no more,
   for they are cut off from thy hand.
Thou has put me in the depths of the Pit,
   in the regions dark and deep (Ps. 88:3–6).

The metaphors of Sheol, pit and death need further comment. When the psalmist speaks of death or of being in Sheol, this is not merely metaphor. Death is dynamic, not static; it is a power rather than a decisive point at the end of a line. It is not "out there," waiting for every human. Rather, it pursues every living being, already on the attack, manifesting itself in sickness, oppression, evil. In short, death is non–life, and all that is opposed to physical, mental and spiritual health belongs to the realm of death. To the extent that the good is absent from life, to that extent death is wielding its influence. The most expressive synonym for death, and one most frequently used in parallelism with it (Pss. 18:5; 49:14; 89:48) is Sheol, or the nether world. This term is many–sided. It designates the "after" (*'ah⁽ᵃ⁾rît*) of those who die (Ps. 73:17), the "place" where are gathered the good and the evil alike (Ezek. 32:17–21; Isa. 14:11–20). Death/Sheol is the relentless pursuer of every human being, for eventually no one can escape this power. And essentially it is non–life, as expressed so well in the cry:

For in death there is no remembrance of thee;
   in Sheol who can give thee praise?
     (Ps. 6:5; cf. 30:9; 88:10–12).

This was the worst aspect of Sheol: there was no contact with the Lord. It was not that Sheol escaped God's reach. He threatens against evildoers in Amos 9:2: "Though they dig into Sheol, from there shall my hand take them." But the *effective* presence of the Lord is lacking in Sheol. That is why Job in his torment could yearn for Sheol as a respite where at least he would be safe from the blows of the Lord (Job 3:11–19; 10:18–22; 14:13). If one were to express this positively, one would say that to live is to praise God (to be in effective contact with him). There is a compact German expression for this: *Leben ist Loben* ("to live is to praise").

Psalm 22 provides an excellent introduction to the language that is typical of the lament. The psalmist is threatened by the bulls of Bashan, dogs, a company of evildoers, the sword, the horns of wild oxen; "poured out like water," "my tongue cleaves to my jaws." What is happening? It has been remarked that all this could not happen to one person in a whole lifetime, much less in an individual occurrence. Such is the language of the lament. It evokes a whole spectrum of evil, without providing the details of the specific distress of the one who is praying. Urgency begets extravagance. The language takes on a range of meaning relevant to countless persons, although their particular agony is different from that of the psalmist. In every case it is a matter of life or death, or better, non–life.

This language also testifies to the reality reflected by the prayers. Real experiences of life, with all their hurt, lie behind the explosive words. We cannot dismiss these words as merely poetic metaphor. In a very real way, death has gripped the psalmist with all its force. This is an honest lament, expressed in dialogical form to the Lord. And it is astounding dialogue—so much so that many are inclined to back off from addressing the Lord in the vivid manner of the laments: Why? How long? Arise! Awake! Indeed, as Claus Westermann has pointed out, the biblical lament has all but disappeared in Christian prayer.[6] In many instances it has been tamed and transformed into an acknowledgment of sinfulness. The psalmist is not averse to acknowledging personal sin and human infidelity. But the issues of life are larger than this, and the psalmist will also challenge God. Can the Lord of all be indifferent to the personal loyalty and integrity of the psalmist or the people (Pss. 10, 35, 74)? Let him look to it! It is relatively rare that "Christian" prayers are as forthright. They have lost the sting of the biblical lament, under the guise of not rebelling against God. The psalmist's faith has been interpreted by some as rebellion. Supposedly, Christian motives should be at work: a Christian is not to express a rebellious sentiment, but to bow to the will of God. This is stoicism, and "keeping a stiff upper lip"; it is not Christianity. It is surely significant that Mark 15:34 reads "My God, my God, why hast thou forsaken me?"—the cry of Jesus is the opening line of Psalm 22! While it is true that resignation to God's will is a virtue, it does not exclude a certain wrestling with God, a vigorous dialogue with him. In fact, it is only great faith that makes this possible, and the greater the struggle, the greater the resignation may be. There should be no scandal taken at the extreme language of the psalmist, or of Job or Jeremiah for that matter.

The "confessions" of Jeremiah are in the same mood as the laments. This prophet has revealed more than others the personal sufferings he had to endure—despite the assurances of the Lord to be with him (Jer. 1:8,18–19). Parenthetically, one may observe that Jeremiah is not the author of the Book of Lamentations, which is not to be confused with laments. The lamentation is an expression of grief over a calamity that is not reversible, whereas the lament is an appeal to God's compassion to intervene and change a desperate situation. Jeremiah poured out his feelings in several magnificent poems (Jer. 11:18—12:6; 15:10–21; 17:12–18; 18:18–23; 20:7–18), which have come to be called his "confessions." In two of these a rather hard response is forthcoming from the Lord. In Jeremiah 15:15–21, the Lord sidesteps the complaint by telling the prophet that if he reforms, that is, converts and settles into the work God has in mind for him, his mission will be renewed (in words that repeat his initial calling in 1:19): "they will fight against you, but they shall not prevail against you, for I am with you to save you and deliver you" (Jer. 15:20). The reply to the complaint of 12:1–4 is much sterner. Jeremiah expresses his anger and grief over the anomaly of the prosperity of the wicked—a reasonable complaint in the light of all that he had to suffer. And the reply of the Lord is classic:

> If you have raced with men on foot,
> and they have wearied you,
> how will you compete with horses? (Jer. 12:5)

Jeremiah receives word that his present trials are as nothing compared to those that await him.

In the introductory chapter attention was called to the remarkable note of certainty with which most laments conclude. It was suggested there that the change in mood was due to an oracle of salvation or deliverance, uttered by one of the temple personnel. However it is to be explained, the fact of the change is of great importance. It means that there is a basic movement in the lament from complaint to praise. These two poles of human existence are united. The complaint is an appeal to divine compassion; when the Lord responds, praise is in order. This sequence of things, it has been pointed out, underlies the presentation of Israel's own historical experience in the exodus and other key events. It is most succinctly expressed by the sequence of events in Judges 2: infidelity, punishment, cry for help, deliverance through a savior–judge. In the lament Israel found a wholesome form for the expression of grief, a movement from brokenness to wholeness.

Walter Brueggemann ("The Formfulness of Grief," *Interpretation* 31 [1977] 263–275) has developed this theme and compared it, by way of contrast as well as similarity, to the several stages which Elisabeth Kübler–Ross detected in hospital patients in her book, *On Death and Dying.*[7] The first step, the denial and isolation faced by a sick person, is not really matched by the psalmist who, even in a lament, starts from a covenantal context; he is in dialogue with the Lord. But the second stage, of anger and rage, has its counterpart in the lament, where anger plays an important role. Thirdly, Kübler–Ross notes the "bargaining" instituted by the patient who will exemplify "good behavior." The biblical parallel to this is the motifs as to why the Lord should intervene (cf. Ps. 24:20–21). Fourthly, the sense of depression and worthlessness can be illustrated from Psalm 22:6, "I am a worm, and no man." However, the psalmist is constantly in dialogue with the Lord, and the depression yields to petition. Finally, the stage of acceptance in the patient corresponds to the motif of the certainty of having been heard (cf. Ps. 6:9). While there are significant differences between the analysis of Kübler–Ross and the components of the biblical lament, the important fact is that in both a change is brought about. We have already seen that the change in the psalmist is probably to be attributed to an oracle of salvation proclaimed by one of the temple personnel. The change in the patient can be effected also by some word of encouragement, of consolation, perhaps a gesture, a sign of sympathy. In both instances, one may speak of the "formfulness of grief."

Psalm 22 was mentioned earlier as an example of extravagant language and imagery in the lament. It will naturally come to mind for Christians who are aware of Mark 15:34, where Jesus is portrayed as proclaiming the first line of Psalm 22, "My God, my God, why has thou forsaken me?" This psalm makes eminently good sense in the context. Jesus was himself a Jew whose piety and understanding of God were nourished by the religious heritage expressed in the temple liturgy, where the psalms were used. How is one to correlate the literal meaning of Psalm 22:1 with the meaning it has in Mark? The speaker of Psalm 22 is one who has been driven to a despair over the absence of God and the terror of suffering. The suffering one is not speaking of someone else, and certainly not predicting another's passion. The suffering is too real for that, and there is nothing in Psalm 22 to suggest that it is a prediction. But the early church was able to see a larger dimension than that of the author of the prayer. That is to say, it understood Jesus as suffering with all who suffer; his passion is redemptive for all. Desolation and trial are his appointed path, just as others have also walked. He sums up in himself the suffering of all persons, and this beautiful psalm becomes the vehicle of his expression of abandonment and faith together. All suffering is a reflection of a primeval suffering which came to its full accomplishment in the passion of Jesus. Hence not only Psalm 22, but Psalm 69, passages from Jeremiah, and other books, come to be used in the New Testament passion narratives.[8]

How is one to reconcile violence and prayer? This question arises because of a prominent feature in the lament: the enemies of the psalmist. Apart from the knotty problem of the nature of the persecution inflicted by these enemies, is the repeated desire to see God wreak vengeance upon these hostile powers. Examples of vengeance are too numerous to mention; let such psalms as 58:6–9; 109; 137: 7–9 suffice. Violence and vengeance, in the Psalter and in the Bible generally, put off many people. Some may even claim that the Bible authorizes revenge and retaliation. Or one might argue that Christian ideals (hardly practice!) transcend such realities. These objections miss the point. Desire for retribution and violence are in fact part of the human condition. They find expression in the Bible (New Testament as well as the Old, it may be added), and it is incumbent upon the reader of the Bible to come to terms with them. What can be said?

First, the reader has to understand and sympathize with the situation that calls forth such vengeance. In the biblical perspective, the Lord is a just God. If evil people flaunt their wickedness (Ps. 73:9, "they set their mouths against the heavens, and their tongue struts through the earth"), they are to be punished by him. Otherwise, where is his justice? Is he to remain inactive when the poor are oppressed by the wicked (Pss. 7:9; 14:4; 71:4)? His intervention must take place now, in this life, the only life that the Israelite knew. Hence the agony of the speaker in Psalm 73, whose "feet had almost stumbled," when he saw the prosperity of the wicked. Justice demands that the wicked be punished. Let it not be thought that the talion law ("an eye for an eye, a tooth for a tooth") was conceived in a harsh manner. This was just the opposite of excess. It demanded equity in which the punishment fit the crime. Thus the excesses of mutually destructive warfare between families and tribes could be averted.

Secondly, the nature of the language should be understood. The very description of the enemies and their machinations gives them a hue of absolute evil. The language used to describe them is so conventional that it is impossible to identify the enemies in the psalms. Some understand them to be primarily personal opponents of the psalmist, who have falsely accused him, and seek to bring him to judgment. Others think that the enemies are magicians (cf. Pss. 7:13ff.; 10:7ff.) who weave spells against the psalmist. They have been given also a political interpretation: people who are friendly with the Greek ruling class, and opposed to the pious who are faithful to the Lord. Or are they the rich who exploit the poor, such as we know from the time of Amos? A mythological interpretation has also been proposed: that the enemies are mythical powers, not human beings.

The language used of these enemies is very broad: mockers, liars, hypocrites, men of blood. They are false, bold, and tyrannical. It emerges that this is not a description of a concrete reality, but a picture of utter godlessness and the power of evil. Human beings are being described, but the conventional language surpasses reality; a model evil, a type, is being presented here. Whence comes this stylization and schematic presentation? Exaggeration hardly explains it; otherwise, one could expect more variations in the descriptions.

The schematization may derive from the liturgical language, which tends towards the typical. The picture of the just person is not the result of an examination of conscience; it emerges from the ideals that a just person is supposed to incorporate, as well as from the basic loyalty that marks one's life. Similarly the picture of the evil person rests upon a classic conception of the embodiment of evil, rather than on the personal oppression experienced by the psalmist. The requests for vengeance are themselves stylized, and one may suspect the influence of the old curse formulas which formed part of the feast of covenant renewal.

Psalm 139 provides an example of the importance of analyzing the language of violence. After an intense meditation upon God's presence and care, the psalmist continues:

> O that thou wouldst slay the wicked, O God,
>   and that men of blood would depart from me,
> men who maliciously defy thee,
>   who lift themselves up against thee for evil!
> Do I not hate them that hate thee, O Lord?
>   And do I not loathe them that rise up against thee?
> I hate them with perfect hatred;
>   I count them my enemies (Ps. 139:19–22).

Both the characterization and the rejection of the wicked are clear. They are the object of the psalmist's hatred. Yet these statements have a direct thrust towards fidelity to God: your enemies are my enemies. This is in effect a statement of loyalty. One might object to the ease with which the identification of God's enemies are made (a universal human failing!). But when one recalls the basic notion of justice in this life, the categorization of good and evil becomes almost inevitable. Neither is the psalmist complacent about personal integrity and loyalty, as the last verses (23–24) show: "Try me!"

An important final point should be made. Perhaps some will remain unconvinced by the previous considerations. Feelings of hatred and revenge seem to be out of place in their prayers. The uneasiness stems from the way in which they pray the psalms. The usual way of using the Psalter in prayer is to identify with the words of the psalmist. When these are sentiments of praise and hope, the psalms become the vehicle of one's personal aspirations. The difficulty arises with prayers of revenge and violence, with which one cannot identify. Is another approach possible? Yes, *hear* the word! Hear the agony and even the sinful violence of human beings—in the context of prayer. These expressions of rage exemplify the demonic in every human heart. These feelings of revenge are not rare or unknown; everyone has experienced them. When they are heard in prayer, they serve to illuminate our own feelings, and even to accuse us of our own acts of vengeance. This can be a salutary way of dealing with psalms of violence. They can judge the violence that lurks in our own hearts. It would be foolish to excise parts of the psalms for the sake of an effete, "proper," liturgical piety. There is an unmistakable air of unreality about such a procedure. At stake, too, is a deeper principle: Can we afford to be selective about our biblical canon? In recent biblical scholarship the issue of a canon within the canon has emerged. That is to say, a given book or books become the key to the interpretation of the whole canon. This procedure is a doubtful one theologically. It fails to attend to the whole spectrum of the biblical word. In a similar way, the men and women who live in a world marked by violence and revenge, should not fail to confront these same realities in the psalms.

CHAPTER FOUR

THE CONTRIBUTION OF THE PSALMS
TO TODAY'S PRAYER STYLE

Although the entire Bible provides fruitful models for prayer, pride of place must be given to the "praises" of Israel, as the official Hebrew title of the Book of Psalms puts it. Our treatment of the psalms thus far has attempted to underline theological insights that came to be expressed in these Israelite prayers. Now we wish to focus on certain presuppositions in Israelite prayer as exemplified in the psalms. We are asking the question: What is it about the psalms that is essential for prayerful communion with God? This question is not as broad as it might at first seem. We do not intend to give an abbreviated overview of Old Testament theology; naturally, Israel's theology forms the background of its prayer. But we would search rather for certain qualities, certain basic approaches to reality. These are the presuppositions of Israel at prayer; they are at the same time vital to our own living experience today, especially if we live somehow out of the biblical tradition. The question, "How did the Israelite pray?" has a bearing on the question, "How does one pray?"

It is a striking fact that so few people *learn* to pray. Perhaps it is assumed that prayer is so personal that it cannot be learned. But more often than not it is reduced to a specific kind of prayer, namely petition. Or one is given a "prayer book," and one repeats the prayers contained therein. People who have lived out of the biblical tradition have indeed used the psalms as their prayers, but this is not the same as learning to pray. The Psalter is not merely a collection of prayers; it is, as Christoph Barth puts its, "a *school* of prayer." That is to say, it is a book from which one can learn what prayer means, and even, Barth goes on to say, "how to pray in the right way." Presumably there may be several such ways. We wish merely to school ourselves in prayer by considering certain features of the psalms.

THE REALITY OF DIVINE PRESENCE

Israel conceived of the Lord as dwelling in the heavens, above the firmament (1 Kings 8:49). But he had become present to Israel in a particular way. Deuteronomy put this in terms of his name (Deut. 12:5, 11, 14). He might be in heaven, but his name dwelt in the Jerusalem temple. Let us not see this as nominalism (which it might be for us). For Israel, the name is the person. Admittedly, this distinction between presence above the firmament and in the temple never became the topic of speculation among the Israelites; it was simply accepted as reality. The Lord could not be imaged, but his residence among his people was upon the ark of the covenant, his footstool or throne. Zion, the place of his choice, became idealized in the biblical tradition. The priestly tradition emphasized the "glory" of the Lord, the tabernacling (*Shekinah*) within Israel. Israel was aware of the divine transcendence, but also of immanence, in line with the words attributed to Solomon (1 Kings 8:27–28): "But will God indeed dwell on the earth? Behold, heaven and the highest heaven cannot contain thee; how much less this house which I have built! Yet have regard to the prayer of thy servant and to his supplication, O Lord my God, hearkening to the cry and to the prayer which thy servant prays before thee this day." No matter the theological problems inherent in the manner of the presence of God with his people, Israel knew that he was present to them.

The immediacy of this presence is characteristic of the psalms. The Lord is acclaimed in procession:

> God has gone up with a shout,
>   the Lord with the sound of a trumpet (Ps. 47:5),

> Ascribe to the Lord the glory due his name;
>   bring an offering, and come into his courts! (Ps. 96:8).

These lines vividly portray the dramatic scene of a procession of the ark ("gone up," i.e., mounted the throne), and the attendant activity of the worshipers. In view of what we have said above about liturgy in the psalms, it would seem that modern liturgical prayer is challenged by the dramatic style of biblical prayer to go through but also beyond a mere service of the word. Celebration, not passivity, is called for, because the Lord is present among his people.

The reality of divine presence is illustrated by the complaint concerning divine absence. If the Lord "hides his face," living things are undone (Ps. 104:29), or the psalmist is struck with terror (Ps. 30:7). One of the frequent gibes leveled at the believer is: "Where is your God?" (Pss. 42:3,10; 79:10; 115:2). But in point of fact, the Lord is never so absent that he cannot be present to the outcry of the psalmist, even after he has "hidden his face":

> To thee, O Lord, I cried;
>> and to the Lord I made supplication:
> "What profit is there in my death,
>> if I go down to the Pit?" (Ps. 30:8–9)

In any case, no matter how the presence and absence of the Lord flickered in and out of life, the writer of Psalm 139 captured the basis of Israelite prayer:

> Even before a word is on my tongue,
>> lo, O Lord, thou knowest it altogether.
> Whither shall I go from thy Spirit?
>> Or whither shall I flee from thy presence? (Ps. 139:4,7)

The presence of the Lord is an *active* presence. Communion through prayer *moves* Him, just as we move each other in any interpersonal relationship. The Lord can "repent" of the evil or good he intended to do (Jer. 18:8–10; Jon. 3:9). All that occurs, good or evil, is his doing. This serene indifference to secondary casuality is perhaps the point at which modern man is farthest from biblical man. Our scientific knowledge, our historical consciousness, seem to block us out from such an intimate reaction to divine presence. We are too sophisticated to accept at face value the explanation that a person might offer for the action of God in personal life. But how little progress the theist has made in explanation of God and his will! The distinction between the absolute and permissive will of God relative to the evil turns and tragedies which we experience has hardly brought us ahead of the biblical view. Indeed, we may have lost the sense of the direct, but always mysterious, action of God which the people of the Bible felt. The closest parallel to it would be a profound sense of providence, a trust in the guidance of God, that would afford the basis of a dialogue with him, and also allow for divine freedom. But this providence should not be allowed to blur the reality and mystery of evil in human experience; one must still somehow contend with the God of Amos: no evil befalls a city that the Lord has not done (Amos 3:6), and with the God of Isaiah (Isa. 45:7), who creates woe as well as makes weal. The post–biblical man of prayer, be he Christian, Jew or Muslim, must retain some sense of the biblical "I–thou" relationship with God, no matter how he explains divine causality.

PRAYING OUT OF A TRADITION

A second characteristic of the psalms is this: Israel prays out of her own tradition, her own history, her own experience. A whole lifetime, whether of the individual or the nation, is brought to bear upon one's present experience of God. It is not necessary that the events of the past match the needs of the present. It is just that the present always seems to have some continuity with the past; it is as if no one comes to the Lord in a vacuum.

Thus, in the songs of praise, there is a response to the saving acts of God in Israel's history. The identity of the God with whom the people commune is established by his actions in history and also in creation:

> Praise the name of the Lord,
>> give praise, O servants of the Lord . . .
> For the Lord has chosen Jacob for himself,
>> Israel as his own possession . . .
> Whatever the Lord pleases he does,
>> in heaven and on earth,
>> in the seas and all deeps.
> He it is who makes the clouds rise at the end of the earth,
>> who makes lightnings for the rain
>> and brings forth the wind from his storehouse . . .
> Who in thy midst, O Egypt,
>> sent signs and wonders
>> against Pharaoh and all his servants (Ps. 135:1–9).

There is an ability shown here to enter into creation and personal history and return them to God in praise. The world declares the glory of God (Ps. 19), and the Israelite savored this revelation of him in the world, a world that was being continually created, since all living things were dependent upon the divine breath for their very existence (Ps. 104:29–30). This attitude to creation is deeper than the pragmatic understanding of ecology that tugs at the heart of modern man. It shares in the response of creation itself to its maker (Job 38:7).

In the laments also there is an awareness that one is not addressing a strange God, but rather the God who has revealed himself in the past:

> In thee our fathers trusted;
>> they trusted, and thou didst deliver them.
> To thee they cried, and were saved;
>> in thee they trusted, and were
>>> not disappointed (Ps. 22:4–5).

> We have heard with our ears, O God,
>> our fathers have told us,
> What deeds thou didst perform in their days,
>> in the days of old (Ps. 44:1).

The sacred history formed the basis of Israel's understanding of itself in relation to the Lord, and the memories of the tradition came to easy expression in prayer.

It is to be expected that today's prayers must also be rooted in something, an historical experience, a personal agony, or some feature of the community with which one is identified. This is part of the defining of who God is, a necessary factor in prayerful activity. What is there in common between God and one's self? What of his history, with his creatures, the experience of creation, the personal experiences that one has shared with him and through him?

IMAGERY

Another important characteristic of the psalms is the peculiar quality of their imagery. They share this, of course, with the rest of the Bible, but it deserves to be underlined from the point of view of prayer. First of all, it may even be advanced as an objection to modern use of the psalms: biblical imagery is too far out, too strange for the person of twentieth-century culture. There is a certain validity to such an objection. The imagery of any culture is itself strange to those of another culture. In a sense the strange culture has to be "learned" if it is to speak at all. There is no escape from this. For example, the metaphorical use of "horn" needs explanation. It is a symbol of strength and of dignity. If it is lifted up, there is victory and prosperity (Pss. 89:24; 92:10; 112:9), but it can also be cut off as a sign of defeat (Ps. 75:11). The Lord can be called the "horn of salvation" (Psalm 18:2), because he is a saving power. However, once the image is learned by the reader, it poses no problem, and it introduces one into an enriching concept of reality by stretching one's imagination. Moreover, western culture has significant roots in the Bible; our literature has been considerably influenced by "Bible English" and biblical metaphor. We are not so insensitive to an imagery that has seeped into our cultural tradition. If we were to grant the force of the objection, we would end up illiterate, biblically and culturally. It is surely an exaggeration to claim that the imagery of "The Lord is my Shepherd" cannot be absorbed by a city dweller who has never seen a sheep. The outreach of the imagery of the poets and writers of our own age is often more difficult to understand and assimilate, than the imagery of the Bible.

However, there is one aspect about the language of the psalms and ern readers. Certain key terms are too easily overlaid with later of the Old Testament which does constitute some difficulty for modreligious or cultural concepts that do not square with the biblical meaning. Perhaps the most obvious example is the word, "soul," which is frequently used to translate the Hebrew *nepeš* (Pss. 103:1; 104:1). Instinctively the reader will interpret from the well-known western categories of soul and body, and impose these upon the text. But they are foreign to the Old Testament. What is translated as "soul" is more appropriately rendered as "person." There is no contrast between soul and body in the Hebrew Bible. If anything, flesh and spirit are contrasted, but these categories do not pertain to the living composite. They indicate, respectively, what is human, limited and weak, as opposed to what is divine and strong (cf. Isa. 31:3). Another key word is *ḥesed,* often rendered as (loving) kindness. But this is a pale reflection of the covenantal love and loyalty that is its primary connotation. Similarly, the word, "righteousness," or "justice" (*ṣdq*) suggests to the modern reader the legal background which the

word has in our culture, and an absolute ethical norm against which
human conduct is to be measured. But the Hebrew term, $ṣ^edāqāh$,
indicates the standard for a relationship, between humans and between
God and humans. Thus, Yahweh's justice is manifested in deeds
which deliver Israel (cf. Judg. 5:11, RSV "triumphs" renders a more
literal "deeds of righteousness"; Isa. 45:8, where righteousness and
salvation are in parallelism). In the psalms particularly the Lord's
righteousness becomes the object of prayer and proclamation (Ps.
22:31, RSV "deliverance"; 98:9). When Abraham believed in the
Lord, it was reckoned to him as righteousness (Gen. 15:6). That is
to say, he was in a right relationship to God. These are only a few
examples of the dangers that lurk in the Psalter for the casual reader.
But it is to be hoped that the serious reader will take pains to overcome these obstacles and open the way to a more correct understanding.

Secondly, I would like to argue more positively that biblical
imagery simply retains its validity, despite cultural differences. It is,
in a sense, transcultural. In the several millennia during which the
Bible has been transmitted throughout the world, it has survived in all
these varied cultural areas. This fact has been served by a certain
accommodation on the part of those who have received the Bible. But
it is enough to suggest the importance of the Bible for a universal
frame of reference. No other work has survived translation (and
explanation!) and exercised a steady appeal across the face of the
earth. In this respect, biblical language has simply become unique,
and its imagery accepted. If one turns to the wide range of prayers
that have been authored in modern times, from Thomas A Kempis
to Malcolm Boyd or Thomas Merton, one begins to appreciate a certain universalism in biblical imagery. This is not to be exaggerated, as
though biblical imagery has an intrinsic advantage that cannot be
matched elsewhere, or as though modern prayers are not also suitable.
But it must be admitted that post-biblical expression has not been
able to escape severe cultural limitations which have quickly stamped
it as dated and particular. In contrast, biblical imagery still has power.
The waters, the flood, the depths, the pit (Pss. 69; 130) are images
that are still meaningful. We have all been in such straits, and the
words of Psalm 66 can be easily made our own:

Thou didst bring us into the net;
  thou didst lay affliction on our loins;
thou didst let men ride over our heads;
  we went through fire and through water;
yet thou hast brought us forth to a
  spacious place (Ps. 66:11–12).

Many images of course, will not fit into modern cosmology and physics. But there is no need to be put off by the biblical "three–story universe," the heavens, earth, and abyss below. One does not read the poems to learn about science, but to be moved into the world of God and his presence. The psalms are dynamic; they appeal to the whole person, not just the mind, and they appeal especially to the imagination. One must beware of merely looking for the idea, and neglecting the coloring, the emotional hue, in which the idea is expressed. The thought has to work on the reader through the concrete form of its expression. This is the difference between reading the catechism and the Bible. The catechism has distilled basic data into questions and answers. The Bible captures the ebb and flow of God's history with humankind, the concrete way in which the experience of God has been expressed. One does not live by ideas alone. To say that God is benign, watching over his children, is really not the same thing as saying "The Lord is my shepherd" (Ps. 23). The issue is less "what," than "how." The psalms open up to us the particular qualities of God as spelled out in human experience.

This means also that we have to learn to yield to the power of the poems, to identify with the writer, and allow reactions to take place within ourselves. The poet, Rainer M. Rilke, has said that as one spends time with a book, there arises tenfold more than was actually expressed in it; one reads one's own memories and thoughts along with it. This is quite true; we are always reading ourselves, our affections and experiences, into the works we confront. We have all had the experience of a deeper reaction and understanding to a literary work in a second, later, reading, as opposed to a first reading. We never remain, at least need not remain, the same when we repeat a reading.

Repetition, in fact, is built into the psalms. The phenomenon of parallelism, so characteristic of Hebrew poetry, is an important factor in the language. The poetic lines are arranged in such a way as to strike a balance. One line will be paralleled by another that is synonymous in thought, so that one repeats in other words what has already been affirmed ("synonymous parallelism," Ps. 51:3–4). Or one line may be in contrast to another ("antithetic parallelism," Ps. 20:7–8), but both lines say the same thing. The simple affirmation is strengthened by differing points of view. Sometimes the parallelism is less rigid, the second or even the third line may merely develop the thought of the first line (Ps. 23:1). Parallelism serves two ends in prayer. It frequently clarifies or expands an image that may not be immediately obvious to the reader. But even more important is the opportunity it provides for a more contemplative approach to the psalm. One lingers longer over the affirmation, and one is able to savor more fully its meaning.

RELEVANCE?

There is no adequate answer for one who judges the aptness of prayers solely on the criterion of "relevance." Like the word, the criterion is too slippery. What is relevant for one person may not be relevant for another. Prayer is an intensely personal matter. The one who prays brings to the psalms a personal way of looking at God and the world—preconceptions that often differ from those of the Bible. In itself, prayer is a free thing, not to be coerced or limited. There are no "necessary" prayers for anyone; only prayer is necessary. But modern prayer forms, however inspiring, have their own cultural limitations, and in many instances begin to pall. In contrast, the Psalter has stood the test of time. The psalms are still recited, whether this be due to convention or to law. For a worshiping community they have a history. It is not too romantic to consider that they were the spiritual staple of Augustine, Luther, Calvin, and Merton, not to mention Jesus Christ and the people of Israel. To put the case more broadly, we have argued that the psalms, with all the cultural limitations they have, are more transcultural than most other prayers. If a test is needed, one should just try a Mesopotamian lament or hymn! For all the specific Israelite world view (on death, life, salvation history), these prayers bear on the fundamental stance of human beings before God. The question of Augustine is pertinent to all. In the *Confessions* (X,6) he asks, "What do I love when I love my God?"

Augustine and others have discovered the answer in the psalms, and in the God who is described therein.

A Christian cannot deny that he or she brings a perspective to the psalms that differs from that of the ancient Israelite. But need it be in opposition to the sense inherent in the psalms? A fundamental distinction should be made here between christocentric and Christian reading. A christocentric interpretation means that one reads the psalms with direct reference to Jesus Christ. While such an approach has many illustrious sponsors, there is a certain arbitrariness about it; it flattens out the Old Testament, reducing it to a Christian dimension. Jesus Christ is the focus of the New Testament, not the Old. In Christian terms, it is the Father of Jesus Christ who is the focus of the Old Testament. A christocentric reading is too simplistic—the Old Testament does not directly deal with Jesus Chrst—and it fails to come into the psalms at the level on which they were written, at the level in which the literal historical sense of these prayers is meaningful. One might as well pray from the *Imitation of Christ,* if one is going to insist on a direct reference to Christ. An honest approach to the psalms begins where they are. It may be added that Jesus himself prayed the psalms out of his own tradition; he was hardly interested in a "Christian" point of view. Christian liturgy itself speaks of an approach to the Father *through* the Lord Jesus Christ.

Still, a Christian might insist that he or she is not an Israelite, and hence is really unable to pray these psalms at the level on which they were written. Truly, everyone stands in a tradition that has developed beyond that of the psalms. Hence one can speak of a Christian reading of psalms. But the important move here is to establish the nature of the continuity between the Old Testament and the New. Ideally, this approach would honor the meaning inherent in the biblical text, and then go on to expand it in a fuller meaning without arbitrariness. Thus when the psalmist speaks of sin, of distress, of salvation, of the puzzle that God is, one can fit this, in a continuous way, into the larger dimension of one's own (Christian or otherwise) experience. While this perspective goes beyond, it continues what is in the text; a different nuance is added, but the meaning of the psalm is taken seriously.

It is well to pray on several levels, and hence to remain alert to the historical meaning of the text, lest it becomes flattened out in a later perspective. Only in this way can one profit from the balance, and even the correction, which the Old Testament offers to the New, or better, to many Christian interpretations of the Bible. Thus some Christians live too easily with the truths of Christian eschatology, resurrection and eternal life. They might conclude, for example, that the Old Testament perspective on death and Sheol has simply no bearing on their understanding of life and death. This attitude is mistaken. Only a deep and firm confrontation with such Old Testament realities will enable them to see the New Testament doctrine in proper perspective. A failure to appreciate the Old Testament view often lies behind a shallow view of Christian doctrine. Not infrequently a Christian has been heard to wonder how it was possible for the Israelite to believe when there was no blessed immortality, no "heaven or hell." Such an understanding is tragic because it reduces religion, and a faith–full relationship to God to a matter of future reward. The true nature of faith is illustrated in the Israelite world, where God was taken seriously on his own terms, regardless of future life. The Lord is the one who brings down to Sheol and brings back (2 Sam. 2:6); immortality was his grant. But even if he did not, there was always the relationship of faith which was to permeate this life. The Israelite welcomed the possession of Yahweh as a part of this world. His faith was not keyed to one half of reality, the next world, but to this world, in which the Lord revealed himself. Dietrich Bonhoeffer's perceptive remarks are pertinent here: "My thoughts and feelings seem to be getting more and more like the Old Testament, and no wonder, I have been reading it much more than the New for the last few months. It is only when one knows the ineffability of the Name of God that one can utter the name of Jesus Christ. It is only when one loves life and the world so much that without them everything would be gone, that one can believe in the resurrection and a new world. . . . I don't think it is Christian to want to get to the New Testament too soon and too directly."[9]

JOB

CHAPTER FIVE

STRUCTURE AND SEQUENCE

One can hardly read Paul's challenging question to the Corinthian community, "Where is the wise man?" (1 Cor. 1:20) without recalling that he was himself the heir of a rich wisdom tradition. He, at least, must have known the whereabouts of the wise man: in the books of Proverbs, Job and Ecclesiastes, and among the Apocrypha, Ecclesiasticus (or Sirach) and the Wisdom of Solomon. These books stand in stark contrast to the historical narratives of the Law and the Prophets, where God's actions on behalf of Israel are such a common theme. The sages of Israel moved in another circle, even if they were presumably devout Yahwists. They did not speak of the specific Yahwist beliefs concerning exodus, covenant, and temple. Instead they analyzed human experience and God's creation in an effort to understand the humbler events of daily life. They were conscious that wisdom was an international possession; hence Solomon's wisdom could be compared to that of the people of the East and of Egypt (1 Kings 4:29–34). The wisdom of Mesopotamia (Ahiqar) and the wisdom of Egypt (Amenemope) are actually reflected in the wisdom books, and we shall see that there were international models for the figure of Job as well.

Wisdom has many facets in the biblical tradition. It denotes the practical skills of an artisan, the cleverness of a courtier, the wisdom of a ruler, ethical conduct, even "fear of the Lord." Eventually it comes to be identified with the Torah, or Law (Deut. 4:6–8; Ecclus. 24:23). Within the wisdom tradition there emerged a rather fixed doctrine of retribution which the sages saw at work in reality: a good deed begets good, and an evil deed yields evil. One may say that this is a profound insight into human acts. Sin and evil are somehow corruptive; virtue and the good produce prosperity. Of course, this law ultimately operated under the aegis of the Lord, for nothing escaped his all–pervasive primary causality. Thus one could understand his justice; he would not allow the wicked/foolish to prosper, and he would bless the good/wise. This association between sin and suffering, between virtue and prosperity, runs through all biblical thought (cf. Deut. 30:15–20; Ps. 37, etc.), and not merely the wisdom tradition. But it became the starting point for the Book of Job. To what extent is this view of retribution correct?

The sages seem at times to have been aware of the shortcomings of retribution, and hence of the mystery of divine justice. Thus we read in Proverbs 3 (cf. Hebr. 12:5–6):

> My son, do not despise the Lord's discipline
> or be weary of his reproof,
> For the Lord reproves him whom he loves,
> as a father the son in whom he delights (Prov. 3:11–12).

However, this drastic point of view is not expressed very often by the sages. They were quite aware of the limits of their own wisdom, for they knew that "no wisdom, no understanding, no counsel, can avail against the Lord" (Prov: 21:30). But a fairly rigid understanding of retribution became dominant. It preserved the traditional, and safe, theology concerning the Lord's justice. In the Book of Job, this theology is voiced by the three friends, Eliphaz, Bildad and Zophar. The speeches of Job, who is presumably the protagonist of the author himself, provide a hard test for it. Job even challenges his friends directly in 13:7, "Will you speak falsely for God, and speak deceitfully for him?"

For his purposes, the unknown author took up an ancient story about a non-Israelite, a man named Job. In Ezekiel 14 Job is bracketed with Noah (Gen. 6—9) and with Danel (not the biblical Daniel, but an heroic figure known from the literature of ancient Ugarit) as righteous persons of antiquity. It appears that the story of the righteousness of Job was handed down in a form that chapters 1—2 and 42 still re-echo. These chapters constitute the framework of the book; they tell of the testing of Job and his fidelity throughout his trials. Eventually he was restored by the Lord. Against this background the author develops a lengthy dialogue between Job and his comforters (chaps. 3—31), the speeches of Elihu, a stranger in more ways than one (chaps. 32—37), and the speeches of the Lord Himself (chaps. 38—41). Let us consider this in detail:

The Prologue (1:1—2:13)

The literary structure of chapters 1—2 shows remarkable symmetry:

1:1–5, Job's integrity described

1:6–22, Job's first test	2:1–10, Job's second test
Dialogue of Yahweh & Satan (vv. 6–12)	Dialogue of Yahweh & Satan (vv. 1–6)
Calamities inflicted on Job (vv. 13–19)	Personal suffering inflicted on Job (vv. 7–8)
Job's steadfastness (vv. 20–22)	Job's steadfastness (vv. 9–10)
	2:11–13, Appearance of Job's three friends

This portion of the narrative serves to set up a situation in which an innocent man is suffering. On the basis of chapters 1—2 the reader of the dialogue will be able to accept Job's claim to integrity; the tragedies he suffers are clearly a test, not punishment for wrongdoing. The description of Job as "blameless and upright" is detailed in 1:1–5; then the scene shifts suddenly to the heavenly court (1:6–12). This divine entourage appears in many biblical passages. The Lord does not dwell in splendid isolation; the "sons of God" (Ps. 29:1), or members of his court, are with him. It is to them that Genesis 1:26 ("Let us make man in our image . . .") refers, when the Lord is portrayed as deliberating about the creation of man. Satan, the adversary, is one of these heavenly beings who has his own function to perform ("going to and fro on the earth," 1:7; 2:2). He is *not* the devil of later biblical theology. He may be cynical, even hostile to humans, but he is merely one of the court. His question is a sharp challenge of the Lord's view of Job's integrity: "Does Job fear God for nought?" (1:9). The blessings bestowed upon Job suggest that his piety is "for nought" (*ḥinnām,* a word that the Lord adopts with some satire in the second scene as "without cause," 2:3). It is in his own interest that Job is upright. But Job gives the lie to this. His reaction to the tragedies that engulf his family and his possessions is exemplary: "The Lord gave, and the Lord has taken away; blessed be the name of the Lord" (1:21). The simplicity of these words does not disguise his exalted conception of the Lord, who stands far and beyond any accountability to humans, whose ways are not to be questioned.

In the repetitive style characteristic of Hebrew narrative, the reader again witnesses another scene in the heavens. Satan will not yield his point, and the Lord permits him to strike Job personally with physical disease. But Job remains faithful, as the author carefully notes (2:10). One feels that there is a double edge in this testing. Job, it is true, is on the griddle. But is this not also a test of the Lord? Can he refuse Satan's challenge, as though he were afraid to face a possible defection on Job's part? Is he a god who secures his position with easy gifts to his followers? The author is not concerned to answer these questions, nor does he betray any judgment on the contrast between the steadfast (not "patient"; see James 5:11) Job of the prologue and the rebellious Job of the dialogue. Scholars generally agree that the original Job story ended in the manner of 42:7ff., with Job's restoration. As a whole, then, it presented the trials of a servant who remained faithful to the Lord and was rewarded in the end for his fidelity. Such a story, which exemplifies so neatly the working out of the traditional theory of retribution, has become the backdrop against which the theory will be debated, and its inadequacies underlined.

The Debate (3:1—27:23)

The debate between Job and the three friends, who break their mournful silence (2:13), is triggered by the tempestuous complaint of Job in chapter 3. From here on, he will alternate with Eliphaz, Bildad and Zophar in three cycles of speeches: chapters 4—14; 15—21; 22—27. This sequence breaks down in chapters 22—27, where some kind of textual dislocation has left Zophar without a line, while to Job are attributed some lines that are inconsistent with his point of view. There is no certainty about the way in which the text should be rearranged.

In contrast to the prologue, the dialogue seems to belong to a different world. God is never referred to as "Lord" (12:9 is an exception), but as God (*El, Eloah*) or the Almighty (*Shadday*). Although the participants are all non–Israelite, they speak out of the Israelite tradition of wisdom. God is creator and supreme ruler of all. Nothing escapes his all–pervading causality. His rule is just; he rewards the good and punishes the evil. The friends appeal to what has been handed down by the "fathers" (8:8; 15:18), a tradition of wisdom which Job knows as well as they (12:2–3). Eliphaz stands out more sharply than his companions. His ideas are more distinctive; he begins more tolerantly, although in the end he levels specific accusations against Job (22:5–9). Modern readers find the sequence of the arguments somewhat disconcerting. There is little if any logical connection between the speeches which the parties direct against one another. Yet they cover many aspects relevant to the problem at hand. The three friends address Job. He speaks to them, but also to God; third person discourse about God changes to second person during his speeches. A tragedy is being played out: the friends are defending the justice of God, but with specious arguments; Job is rightly claiming his own integrity, but at the expense of the justice of God.

Commentators are divided over whether Job's lament in chapter 3 merely introduces the dialogue or properly forms part of it in such a way that the friends are seen responding to Job's speeches. In chapter 3 Job never addresses the friends; he simply laments. This can be said to serve as a prelude to the debate which is followed by another soliloquy in chapters 29—31. Job laments that he was ever born and curses the day of his birth. How much more fortunate would he have been to have died in the womb, to "live" in Sheol with its varied inhabitants. The nether world is the great leveler, embracing all from still born to kings, small and great. Several times Job will end his speeches on the melancholy note of Sheol (7:21; 10:21–22; 17:16).

Eliphaz begins his speech (chaps. 4—5) in a tactful and sympathetic manner. He notes that in the past Job was a source of strength to the weak (Job will develop this point at length in chapter 29), and he implies that this is the time for him to put his good advice to work. His question is: "Is not the integrity of your ways your hope?" Of course it is, but Job will understand integrity in a manner different from the three. Eliphaz describes a nocturnal vision about the truth of the human condition: "Can mortal man be righteous before God?" (4: 17). Immediately he puts before Job the proverb "happy is the man whom God reproves" (Job 5:17; see the similar thought at Prov. 3:11–12). If Job turns to God, his restoration will be forthcoming (5:8–25).

Job's reaction is impatience with the "sermon" of Eliphaz. He alone appreciates how miserable his condition is (6:2–7). Despite his confidence in his own integrity, he simply has no more strength (vv. 8–12). He compares the proffered consolation of the friends to the experience of thirsty travellers confronted by a dried-up wadi (vv. 14–23), and challenges them: "make me understand how I have erred" (vv. 24–30). He launches into a description of man's "hard service" and accuses God of hounding him (7:1–16)—although Psalm 8 extols the greatness of man and God's providence over him! What irony! God will not even look away long enough for him to swallow his spittle! (vv. 17–21).

Bildad's vehement reply (8:2–3) lapses into a moralistic lecture concerning God's rewarding of the "blameless" man and his destruction of the "godless" man. This is the traditional theory of retribution, applied as rigorously as a law of nature. Job's reaction (chaps. 9—10) shows how much more sensitive to God and his transcendence he himself is: how can a man be just before God? (cf. 4:17). He knows of God's power as well as they do, but God is beyond any question (such as, how or why) that he can ask; he cannot *see* God (9:11). He complains bitterly about the uneven "contest" he finds himself in (vv. 12–21), and places the responsibility for evil squarely upon God (vv. 22–24). This strong language is followed by a lament (vv. 25–35) concerning the brevity of life and the hopelessness of a confrontation with God ("thou wilt plunge me into a pit," v. 31). He yearns for an "umpire," or arbiter, who might ensure a fair trial. Then he moves from a God of might and justice to a God of compassion and understanding (10:1–13), and he makes a moving appeal to the one who so lovingly created him. But these serene thoughts are followed in verses 14–22 by a realistic appraisal of the way God is actually treating him, concluding with the wish that he had never been born.

If any restraint has been observed by the friends, it disappears now. Zophar makes several accusations against Job and then reads him a lesson concerning God's wisdom (11:1–12). He ends with a homily on the happiness that will come to Job if he repents (vv. 13–20). Job is more than ready to debate the wisdom of God. He ridicules with biting sarcasm the friends' claim to wisdom; what kind of wisdom can account for the just man being made a laughing stock, while "the tents of robbers are at peace?" (12:1–6). Even the beasts know that this is God's order of things, and it is an order that manifests destructive might without any moral considerations (vv. 7–25). Job castigates the friends severely: "will you speak falsely for God?" (13:1–12). He will not be guilty of that; he will be honest and face up to him, because he believes in the divine integrity ("This shall be my salvation, that a godless man shall not come before him," v. 16). Job's faith is high at this point ("I know that I shall be vindicated," v. 18b), and the King James rendition of 13:15 is to be preferred to that of the RSV: "Though he slay me, yet will I trust in him." Job seems to have regained strength; he challenges God to make known his transgressions and questions the divine conduct toward him (vv. 20–28). In chapter 14 he returns to a complaint he voiced in 7:1–10: the brevity and misery of life (14:1–12). Why should God bother with a mortal human being whose days are numbered, who marches inexorably towards death? This is expressed with great beauty and feeling in the passage concerning the tree and man (vv. 7–12), and the delicate wish that God might hide him in Sheol until his wrath is over (vv. 13–17). But there is no hope for human beings (vv. 18–22).

In contrast to his first appearance, the language of Eliphaz is now very sharp; he is shocked by Job's intemperate utterances which only betray his wickedness (15:1–6). Job acts as one omniscient and supremely wise (vv. 7–16). Instead he should listen to the traditions of the ancients, which Eliphaz relates by describing the typical fate of the wicked person (vv. 17–35).

After some preliminary taunts against the repetition of his "miserable comforters" and their unreal claims (16:2–4), Job presents a vivid account of God's hostility towards him (vv. 6–17). The divine attack is savage, comparable to that of a beast (v. 10), a wrestler (v. 12), an archer (v. 13), an opponent armed with a sword (v. 13–14). Job's mourning is not a sign of sin ("My prayer is pure," v. 17), but of his grief over the implacable enmity of God. He then makes a moving appeal in verses 18–22. He is, as it were, a man slain, whose blood cries out to God:

> O earth, cover not my blood,
>   and let my cry find no resting place.
> Even now, behold, my witness is in heaven,
>   and he that vouches for me is on high (16:18–19).

Who is this witness, whose conduct is the opposite of the friends (v. 20), who "would maintain the right of a man with God" (v. 21)? Commentators are not agreed on the answer. Is it God himself, or some mediator in the heavenly court (see also 19:25)? It seems to be God, for Job, here as elsewhere, is playing off God against God, appealing to his compassionate side, as against his omnipotence. Job's speech concludes with a lament that suggests his high hope for a saving intervention will hardly be fulfilled (17:1–16); he begins and ends on the note of death (vv. 1, 16).

After a few taunts at Job (18:2–4), Bildad delivers a speech concerning the inevitable fate of the wicked (vv. 5–21). One has the impression of an academic lesson being read out by an insensitive teacher. Job's reaction indicates how deeply he feels the reproaches of his friends (19:2–5). He then describes once more (vv. 6–12; cf. 16:7–14) the savage attack that God has unfairly mounted against him. The hostile presence of God is balanced against a complaint concerning his absence (v. 7). He lists the many persons, kin and friends, who have abandoned him; they feel no pity for him in his ugly physical condition (vv. 13–22).

At precisely this desperate moment Job passes on to one of the high points of faith in the dialogue (vv. 23–27). He solemnly calls for a permanent recording in stone of what he has to say. Unfortunately verses 25–27 are obscure, due to textual corruption, and have been interpreted in various ways. Christian tradition, as exemplified by Jerome's Vulgate translation, saw here a proclamation of a belief in the resurrection of the body. This can hardly be the case. Elsewhere Job clearly has nothing to look forward to beyond death, and a belief in the resurrection of the body would have influenced his whole argument. But Job does make an act of faith in his ultimate vindication by God, who is here called *gō'ēl*, vindicator or redeemer. The *gō'ēl* was a person, next of kin, whose obligation it was to provide help for the relative in need, such as payment of a debt. God is more than an "umpire" (9:33) or a "witness" (16:19)—he is Job's vindicator. Job lays great emphasis (three times in 19:26–27) on his *seeing* this vindicator. But the time and manner of the vindication are not specified. Could Job be anticipating the theophany of chapter 38—therefore, a vision of God in this life? Such a view does not harmonize with his words in verses 23–24 which mention a *permanent* record; this would be needless if he expects vindication before he dies.

Despite the uncertainties in the text, there can be no gainsaying that Job makes an act of faith in an ultimate vindication by God.

Zophar begins his speech by replying (20:2–3) to the warning with which Job had concluded his dramatic statement of faith (19:28–29). However, his speech is in the typical academic style of his companions: "the triumph of the wicked is short" (vv. 5–11, author's translation) and wickedness is self-destructive (vv. 12–29). Job's discourse in chapter 21 is unique in that he confines his remarks to answering his friends, without addressing God, or uttering a lament. He is intent upon contradicting the unreal understanding of retribution put forth by the friends. The fact is that the wicked receive the goods of this life, and God does not interfere with them. They die as prosperously as they live, and it is no consolation to say that divine justice wreaks vengeance upon their descendants. Eliphaz is now convinced of Job's wickedness (22:2–6), and he goes on to list several supposed "sins" of which Job is guilty—all of them relative to Job's treatment of other human beings (for Job's innocence on this score, see chap. 31). He defends God against indifference, and appeals to Job to come to terms with him by repentance, in order to be restored (vv. 12–30).

In chapter 23 Job offers a soliloquy, addressed neither to the friends nor explicitly to God. The theme is God's absence, despite Job's yearning to find him. He speaks in a mournful tone, but expresses confidence that were he to come before God, his case would be judged fairly and he would be "acquitted for ever" by him (vv. 2–6). This confident style is in marked contrast to his earlier utterances (9:13–21; 13:13–27) about a confrontation with the Almighty, but it has been prepared for by 19:25–27. Even though God is so elusive and difficult to encounter (23:8–9), Job believes "he knows the way that I take; when he has tried me, I shall come forth as gold" (v. 10). Job seems here to accept his situation as a test (contrast 7:18). He makes a strong affirmation concerning his loyal service (vv. 11–12; so much for Eliphaz' accusations in 22:6–9!), and his awareness that God does have plans for him (vv. 13–14). Yet, the presence of the Almighty, even if desired by Job, is a terrifying thing, and Job ends on a sombre note (vv. 15–17). This beautiful chapter has been aptly described as portraying the "dark night of the soul."

Job turns to the topic of God's indifference to the crimes perpetrated by the wicked—his failure to care for those who are sorely oppressed (24:1–17). The following section (24:18–25) is practically illegible. It is textually corrupt, and where certain lines can be "translated," they remain obscure, and seem to contain statements that Job could not have uttered. Hence many commentators attribute these fragmentary lines to Bildad or Zophar, or the verses (18–20 or even 18–25) are regarded as a quotation of the friends. The RSV adopts the latter view, and inserts "You say" before verses 18–20, so that verses 21–25 contain Job's answer to the quotation of the friends. Any reconstruction for these lines remains highly tentative. Bildad's final speech in chapter 25 consists of only five verses. It is basically a restatement of the earlier position expressed by Eliphaz in 4:17 and 15:14. In view of the unsettled character of the text in chapters 24—27, it may be fragmentary, and some look to 26:5ff. as a continuation of 25:2–3.

As the Masoretic text stands, Job begins a speech in 26:1, and no other speaker is introduced until Elihu appears in chapter 32. There is, however, an unusual and clumsy reintroduction of Job ("and Job again took up his discourse, and said") in 27:1 and 29:1. As has already been indicated, several commentators reconstruct the missing speech of Zophar, and also fragments of Bildad, from chapters 26—27.

Job's sarcastic questions to Bildad in 26:1–4 are cutting. In view of Bildad's ignorance and impotence, the following lines (vv. 5–14) can be read as Job's lesson about God's creative activity. This is "the finest cosmological section in the dialogue for scope of imagination and force of language" (R. A. F. MacKenzie).[10] It begins with Sheol (Abaddon) and eventually extends to all of creation: the pole–star ("north" or Saphon), clouds, moon, horizon ("circle"), and pillars of heaven. There is an allusion to the divine battle with Yam (v. 12, ("sea," parallel to "Rahab"; cf. Job 3:8; 9:13), known from Ugaritic sources, and also to Leviathan (cf. 41:1). God's creative action is presented as continuous in 26:5–11, while verses 12–13 refer back to creation in mythological terms. The final verse is filled with wonder at this vision:

> Lo, these are but the outskirts of his ways;
>> and how small a whisper do we hear of him!
> But the thunder of his power who can
>> understand? (Job 26:14).

Job had spoken of creation already in 9:4–10, but chapter 26 is in a class by itself, and compares best with the speeches of Yahweh in chapters 38—41.

The problematical aspects of chapters 24—27 appear again. The unusual introduction of 27:1 is matched in 29:1. Job's stout proclamation, under oath, of his innocence stands by itself (27:2–6). There follows an imprecation upon his "enemy" (vv. 7–12). The final poem "on the portion of a wicked man with God" (vv. 13–23) is difficult to reconcile with Job's attitude. It is not that Job would need to deny that a wicked person also receives harsh treatment! Job, like Ecclesiastes ("the preacher"), simply cannot make any sense of God's dealing with humans. But the language is so conventional, and the theme so frequently on the lips of the friends, that it is more likely attributable to one of them.

The Poem on Wisdom (28)

Chapter 28 stands out in all singularity and beauty, unconnected with the previous or following chapter, but complete in itself. There is no introduction in the Masoretic text, and hence it was understood as part of Job's discourse. Commentators usually regard it as a later insertion either by the author or a later hand because it seems to be such an independent composition, and also to raise a new point of view: "Where is wisdom to be found?" Answer: wisdom, which is with God alone, cannot help human beings to solve the problem under discussion. The style is serene. The topic of the personification of wisdom is in the tradition of Proverbs 8 and Ecclesiasticus 24. The chapter may be termed an "interlude," but this does not really explain its strange appearance here. The refrain in verses 12 and 20, "whence wisdom?" contains the theme. The answer is developed negatively: Wisdom cannot be discovered by mining the earth (vv. 1–6, 9–11); it cannot be seen by keen-sighted birds or strong animals (vv. 7–8); it cannot be bought (vv. 13–19). Wisdom is hidden, even from Death (vv. 21–22; cf. v. 14). The answer comes in verses 23–27: Wisdom is with God alone—he "saw," "declared," "established," "searched out" wisdom. The implication, drawn and developed especially by Gerhard von Rad, seems to be that God placed wisdom in creation; it is not merely a divine attribute. The final verse, which is commonly considered to be an addition, goes in another direction: Wisdom is fear of the Lord. In the total context of the book this makes sense, for it ties in with 1:8 and 2:3.

Job's Soliloquy (29—31)

This long discourse can be seen as a pendant to Job's introductory complaint in chapter 3. It is his final statement, a kind of lament that describes the past (chap. 29), the present (chap. 30) and concludes with an oath of innocence (chap. 31). Job begins with an acknowledgement of the divine presence "in the days when God watched over me" (29:2–6). He notes the honor and prestige he enjoyed in the community (vv. 7–10, 21–25), especially because of his many kindnesses (vv. 12–17). He had every reason for hoping to live on prosperously to a ripe old age (vv. 18–20). The tone of lament takes over chapter 30 in which he describes his present condition by way of contrast to chapter 29. He suffers public reproach, even from the most contemptible (30:1–15). He cries out bitterly about this suffering which God inflicts upon him (vv. 16–22). He cites his own sympathy for his fellows as a motif why the Lord should have intervened favorably (vv. 23–26). His final words (vv. 27–31) about his suffering and loneliness are extremely moving.

Job's last consideration is a bold affirmation of his innocence, modelled upon the oath of innocence, a negative confession in the formulaic style, "If I have done such and such, may this happen to me!" This oath was an ultimate step in legal action. The evidence for innocence might be ambiguous or even lacking, so the oath appealed to God for a verdict. God presumably would see to it that one who swore a false oath would be met by the fate which the culprit had wished upon himself. The *lex talionis,* or talion law, often governed the nature of the penalty (e.g., 31:9–10). Job varies the formula, sometimes saying only, "If. . . ." (e.g., 31:19–20), or omitting the penalty which is implicitly understood (e.g., 31:29–30). Hence not all agree on just how many specific wrongs are enumerated (between twelve and sixteen?). The moral values enshrined in Job's oaths are high. He eliminates lust (vv. 1, 9–12), various forms of injustice and dishonesty (vv. 5–8, 13–15, 38–40), failures against charity (vv. 16–23, 31–32), greed (vv. 24–25), idolatry (vv. 26–28), vindictiveness (vv. 29–30), and hypocrisy (vv. 33–34). Many translations put these in an order different from that of the Hebrew. At least the outcry of Job in verses 35–37 seems to be a natural conclusion to the series of oaths. Job lays down a challenge to God to render a verdict. The accusing indictment of his "adversary" would be his badge of honor and crown (since it would be hopelessly false). This statement is his "signature," literally his *tau* (the last letter of the Hebrew alphabet, and hence Job's last word)—"let the Almighty answer me!"

Elihu (32—37)

Biblical scholars are almost unanimous in claiming that the Elihu speeches are a later addition to the book, and apparently from another hand. The arguments for this are strong ones: The language is significantly different, and the speeches seem to be a reflection on specific points raised in chapters 3—31 (Elihu is fond of quoting Job, e.g., 34:3 and 12:11; 35:6 and 7:20). Elihu appears abruptly after the challenge Job hurls at God in chapter 31; he is not even mentioned in the epilogue. Moreover, he does not really contribute anything substantial to the debate, and even seems to anticipate in 36:22—37:24 the Yahweh speeches that are to follow.

However valid these arguments appear to be, one must still try to understand the role of Elihu within the book as it now stands. The reason for his intervention is the failure of the friends to prove Job wrong (32:3). The end of the debate—and the defeat of the friends —is signalled by the silence of the three, and perhaps even by the total absence of the Zophar speech (as the text presently stands). In contrast to the judgment of the Lord (42:7), Elihu's view is that Job has put God in the wrong (32:2), and his speeches aim to correct this. The absence of any response from Job can hardly be interpreted as a sign of Elihu's victory. For, despite the claims he makes for himself as "perfect in knowledge" (36:4; cf. 37:16!) and possessing the spirit of God (32:8; 33:4), Elihu hardly goes beyond the arguments of the friends. He does underscore the medicinal character of human trials that tame human pride (33:17) and the divine warning (36:9–10) that converts a person from iniquity. But the entire thrust is guided by the traditional theory of retribution represented by the views of the three friends.

Elihu's introduction of himself in 32:6–22 is full of bombast, an *apologia* for his intervention. His formal refutation of Job in 33:8–28 is preceded by a lengthy prelude (33:1–7) that gives further evidence of his verbosity. He develops the ways in which God speaks to a human being—in a dream or through suffering—and portrays the happy fate of a sinner who is converted and restored. In chapter 34 he addresses "wise men" (the friends?) and condemns Job as wicked (vv. 2–9). He defends God's justice (vv. 10–37): as Creator, he watches over all; being Almighty, he need not fear, and will show no partiality; his omniscience allows no evil to go unpunished. In his next speech he attempts to answer Job's question, "how am I better off than if I had sinned?" (35:1–8), and he deals with the problem of unanswered prayer (35:9–24). One can recognize two distinct parts to his final address (36:1—37:24). He reads a lesson to Job about God's just dealings with humankind (36:1–21), and then makes a transition to a long and impressive poem about the wonders shown by God in creation (36:22—37:24).

Yahweh's Speeches and Job's Reply (38:1—42:6)

Job had yearned for the presence of the Lord (9:32–35; 13:22–24; 16:19–22; 23:3–5; 30:20), and had even demanded an answer from him (31:35). Now the Lord speaks from the whirlwind and delivers two addresses concerning his creation. They are hardly what one would expect at this point, although the topic of creation has already appeared many times in the book (9:5–10; 26:5–14; 28; 36:26—37:24). But nothing is said about Job's suffering, or about his guilt or innocence. The Lord challenges Job: "I will question you" (38:3). And questions there are in abundance; there is scarcely an affirmative statement. Four general forms of questions are used: "(do) you know" (38:4–5,18,21,33; 39:1–20; "can/do you" 38:12,31–32, 34–35,39; 39:10–12,19,20); "who does" (38:5,8,25f., 36f.,; 39:5f.); "where" (38:4,19,24). And there is the ironic affirmation of the Lord, "surely you know" (38:5,21). These questions are far from catechetical; they force Job into the mysteries of creation before which he can only say, "I lay my hand on my mouth" (40:4). As Gerhard von Rad has remarked, the Lord lets creation do the speaking for him: the creative act, the mass of the earth, the birth of the sea, sunrise, the ocean deeps, the dwelling of light and darkness, the storehouse of snow and hail, wind, rain and ice, the constellations, clouds and lightning. The animal realm is then surveyed: lion and raven, goat and wild ass, wild ox and ostrich, the horse and hawk. The first speech ends with the challenge with which it began (40:2; 38:2–3). Job, the "faultfinder" (40:2), has a somewhat ambiguous, even if humble, reaction. He does not raise the question of the relevancy of all these questions to his own case. But neither has he been accused of wrong-doing, nor does he admit that he has sinned. Beneath all the questions, this speech makes a clear affirmation: God is involved in his creation, which in its infinite variety remains a mystery to man. A clear infer-ence arises from Job's particular situation: human standards of judg-ment are not adequate to deal with the mysteries of creation—can Job continue with his global attack on God's handling of justice? Job is in over his head; who is he to debate with God?

The final part (40:6—41:34) has been regarded by many as an addition to the work, in particular the long poems on Behemoth and Leviathan. The treatment of these two monsters, while brilliant in itself, does slow down the narrative; the style is didactic, and the question style has all but disappeared. But it has been pointed out how integral these poems are to the structure of the work[11]: The state-ments of the Lord are carefully calculated to surpass, both for quality and quantity, the final plea of Job in chapters 29—31. Without the poems on Behemoth and Leviathan, the Lord's reply would fall short. This kind of pattern, whereby one speaker overmatches another, appears also in the length of the Job speeches in chapters 9—10 and 12—14. Hence there is not sufficient reason to reject the authenticity of 40:6—41:34.

The speech begins as the first one does (40:7 = 38:3), and the Lord continues in a style that deals more pointedly with the issues involved (40:8–14): "Will you even put me in the wrong?" Let Job realize that he cannot be his own vindicator. He cannot control the creation, God's handiwork; only if he could, might he expect to be vindicated. The moral discussion ends abruptly and the Lord delivers the dis-courses about the two animals, the description of which fluctuates between mythological monsters, and real animals. Behemoth (literally, "beasts," a plural form) is used as a proper name here and has been often identified with the hippo, though not all the details fit. Leviathan (Job 3:8; Pss. 74:14; 104:26; Isa. 27:1) is known from Ugaritic literature. This is a seven-headed monster, and the common identifica-tion with the crocodile is uncertain. But the identity is perhaps less well put as an either/or question. There may be a particular animal in mind, but the author has invested these with significant mythological touches. As a result, they are not just two more animals added to those already enumerated in chapter 39. Rather they are to be seen as embodying the powers of chaos. The divine speech is all the more devastating; the Lord is underscoring the divine power which holds chaos at bay, and sustains the order of the world. These puzzling animals are further examples of the inexplicable and the uncontrollable, and the Lord makes the usual sallies against Job (40:15; Hebrew 40:25–32=RSV 41:1–8): "Can you draw out Leviathan with a fishhook? . . . Will you play with him as with a bird?"

Job's reply (42:1–6) goes well beyond his first reaction in 40:3–5. He cries out that the Lord can do everything, that none of his plans can be thwarted, and he admits that he has dealt with things "too wonderful" for himself to understand. In 42:3–4 his responses are in reaction to the ironic questions of the Lord, which are quoted from 38:2–3. The heart of his response lies in 42:5,

> I had heard of thee by the hearing of the ear,
>   but now my eye sees thee.

Hearsay gives way to vision; second–hand report, to immediate experience. Here is the turning point. The Job who steadfastly refused to adopt the easy way out which the three friends provided him with their traditional theology, now abandons himself to the Lord. He has not received from the Lord an "explanation" of the suffering meted out to him; neither has he surrendered his own integrity. He does not confess any sins, even when he says "I repent"; he simply yields to the Lord.

Epilogue (42:7–17)

The Lord now (vv. 7–9) delivers a clear verdict to Eliphaz: "My wrath is kindled against you and against your two friends; for you have not spoken of me what is right, as my servant Job has." Throughout the debate, it was Job who apparently stood under the wrath of God, in the judgment of the friends. But not so! It is they and their narrow theology—narrow as applied to Job—that stand condemned. The irony is ultimate: it is only by Job's intercessory prayer that their sacrifice will avert the divine displeasure.

Many commentators have argued that verses 7–9 refer to an

original dialogue between Job and the friends, which was replaced by the present debate in chapters 3—31. But such a reconstruction remains quite hypothetical, and adds nothing to our understanding of the text as it now stands. Similarly, the "sympathy" of Job's brothers and sisters has been interpreted as part of the old Job story, where the sympathy is of a piece with the silence of the friends in 2:13. At any rate, the scene in 42:11 is to be taken as an element in the restoration of Job

Job's restoration in verses 12–17 consists in doubling the possessions he lost (flocks and herds). Interestingly, no mention is made of his physical cure. The patriarchal flavor of the narrative is suggested in the details about his children and grandchildren, and his ripe old age. It would be a mistake to seize upon Job's restoration as the message of the book, or as a failure of nerve on the part of the author. It stands to reason that Job should be freed from the affliction agreed to by the Lord and Satan in chapters 1—2. But one can not infer that the author is undoing all that he has thus far written. He does not deny that God rewards the just, that material prosperity can be a sign of God's love. Indeed, God's gifts need no explanation; it is their absence that creates problems. After all, there is no intention to deny God's goodness and love, and the restoration is a concrete way of expressing this. Even if the author has merely adopted the ending of the old tradition about "holy" Job, his choice to do so is as deliberate as is his choice to compose a dialogue that shows how complicated the question of reward/punishment really is. One might see a final touch of irony in his retention of a "happy ending," after the debate has shown that such a view, taken by itself, is simplistic. The message of the book is not to be resolved by trumpeting the last lines.

CHAPTER SIX

THE MESSAGE OF THE BOOK

According to Marvin Pope, ". . . there is no single classification appropriate to the literary form of the Book of Job. It shares something of the characteristics of all the literary forms that have been ascribed to it, but it is impossible to classify it exclusively as didactic, dramatic, epic, or anything else. The book viewed as a unit is *sui generis* and no single term or combination of terms is adequate to describe it."[12] But while there is no adequate genre which captures this book, it is well to note the several sub-genres that find expression in it.

One of these is the "lament," already familiar from the Book of Psalms. Indeed, some have spoken of Job as the "dramatization of a lament." Certainly, the lament plays a large role. Job begins and ends with a personal lament (chaps. 3 and 29—31), and his dispute with the three friends frequently takes on the tone of lament (e.g., chaps. 7; 10; 13:13–28; 14; 16—17).

Another important feature of the work is the legal style which it exemplifies. This appears in some of the pointed questions that Job aims at the three friends, as in 6:22–30, where the legal terminology of "ransom," "reprove," "vindication," appears (cf. also 9:32–35; 13:1–12). The importance of this legal terminology is that it underscores the gravity of the debate. Job actually imposes judicial responsibility on the Lord, and his words are to be taken seriously.

Finally, there are wisdom elements scattered throughout the work, such as the proverbial sayings in 5:6–7, and 6:5–6 and elsewhere. Bildad's reference to the "fathers" and their teaching (8:8) is typical of the wisdom approach. In 12:2 Job makes an issue of wisdom, claiming it for himself against the monopoly on it which the three friends seem eager to establish. The approach of all the speakers is that of the Israelite sage; they argue from creation, not from salvation–history.

A recent trend in scholarly interpretation of the Book of Job shows considerable influence from modern literary criticism. Two eminent literary critics, Northrop Frye and Christopher Fry, had already suggested the book belonged to the genre of comedy. J. William Whedbee has argued vigorously for such an interpretation in his "The Comedy of Job," *Semeia* No. 7, *Studies in the Book of Job*.[13] Although comedy is a difficult genre to define, Whedbee's definition is clear and reasonable. Comedy does not exclude tragedy, nor can it be defined by laughter. It consists of two central features: a vision of incongruity (what is ironic, or ludicrous or ridiculous), and a basic story line that ultimately reintegrates the hero into his society.

The so-called "happy ending" in Job illustrates the last point. The epilogue brings Job back to his world, a "comic upturn." Incongruity begins to appear already in the prologue, where the reader is provided with vital information which is not known to Job and his friends. Indeed, God himself is represented as saying to the Satan, ". . . you moved me against him, to destroy him without cause" (2:3). Already, the dark side of God is foreshadowed, and Job will develop this in his speeches in chapters 7, 9, and 12.

Throughout the book irony and ridicule appear. The reader cannot fail to see in the first utterance of Job (chap. 3) the incongruity of the Job of the dialogue with the Job of the prologue. The friends are caricatured—especially by Job. He speaks of silence (with which they began in 2:13) as their true wisdom (13:5). The figure of Eliphaz is a parody of those "wise counsellors" in Israel, such as Ahithophel, Absalom's adviser. When he describes the "ripe old age" of Job (provided Job repents, 5:26; cf. 8:5–7; 11:13–19), he is actually anticipating the epilogue! The stereotyped descriptions of the righteous and the wicked which the friends present are no match for the ridicule with which Job answers them. He unleashes a trenchant attack on their moralizings (12:2–3; 13:12; 16:2–5; 26:2–4). One can thus see in the friends a classical comic figure, the *alazon,* or fool.

However, it is God who is Job's real enemy, and Job parodies divine worship when he refers to Psalm 8 in 7:17–18. He turns the song of praise into a song to the God of terror and destruction (9:2–10). His final words in 31:35–37 are aimed at God, but instead another *alazon* appears, Elihu, the interloper—"an angry young man," as Whedbee calls him, whose platitudes agree with his bombastic style.

The irony in the divine questions of the Yahweh speeches has long been recognized ("where were you . . . ?" cf. 38:2–5; 40:2, 6–14). But there is another edge of irony present in that Job has already anticipated in 9:3–4, 11–12 the apparently insensitive way in which God would act. What does the theophany say to Job? It presents him with a double vision: of God, and also of the world as God sees it (as von Rad had already pointed out, God lets nature do the talking for him here). Whedbee underscores the fact of the two divine speeches and the two replies of Job (40:3–5 and 42:1–6); he calls this a "two-stage movement," from silence to repentance. Job's reaction is really a paradox: he has seen God (42:5), but he also sees that he does not see.

If the literary genre of Job is unique, it is to be expected that the work is unparalleled in the ancient world. This is true, but only up to a certain point. The question of God's justice towards his creatures is an old problem and many traditions have struggled with it. The so–called Sumerian Job ("Man and his God," *ANET,* 589–591) hardly qualifies for the title. Like Job, and most other human beings, he suffers without apparent guilt. When he confesses his wrongdoing, he is restored by his God. Indeed, he could be a model which Job's three friends might have used for their mistaken views! Similarly, the long Akkadian poem, "I will Praise the Lord of Wisdom" (*ANET,* 596–601) is really a song in praise of Marduk, the "lord of wisdom," for having delivered a nobleman from his sufferings. Although the complaint presents some similarity to Job's lament ("who knows the will of the gods in heaven?"), there is nothing of Job's challenge and confrontation with the Lord. Other Mesopotamian works, such as the "Babylonian Theodicy" (*ANET,* 601–604), and the "Dialogue of Pessimism" (*ANET,* 600–601) are more comparable to Ecclesiastes than to Job. The Egyptian works, such as the "Harper's Songs," and "The Man Who was Tired of Life" (*ANET,* 467; 405–407) have a distant similarity to Job. While the theme of the righteous sufferer was not unknown in the ancient Near East, there is no question of the dependence of Job upon any of these works. There was a literary tradition in existence, but the author of Job went his own way, in a peculiarly Israelite style.

It is paradoxical that there is disagreement over the message of the Book of Job. Perhaps this is a sign of its greatness; it illustrates so many aspects of life. Marvin Pope has remarked: "Viewed as a whole, the book presents profundities surpassing those that may be found in any of its parts."[14] The reason for disagreement about the message is that there is no single message; the work is too rich for that. The mysterious relevance of the Lord's speeches in chapters 38—41 is a symbol of the quest for the book's meaning. We are not going to receive any pat answer; but we can be transformed by the experience of confronting the book, as Job was confronted by the Lord.

It is true to say that the purpose of the book is to argue against the traditional theory of retribution; the direction of the dialogue clearly shows this. But is the point of the work merely negative? Or is the author suggesting several considerations on a complex topic, the mystery of which he never finally "solves"? This seems to be the case; several points of view emerge.

The first two chapters raise the question of disinterested piety, a piety that does not depend upon a *do ut des* (I give, in order that you give [to me]) principle. The fact that Job remains steadfast is not as important as the ideal itself. Even had he followed his wife's advice ("curse God and die," 2:9), the issue of disinterested piety is put before the reader in a challenging way.

The Job of the dialogue is sometimes said to be in "contradiction" to the Job of the prologue. Of course he is, in the sense that there is new development; an innocent man will confront the traditional view of reward and punishment. The author has moved to a new terrain where the issue of traditional retribution is made an issue of debate. The terrain is that of wisdom, of legal procedure, and even of prayer (Job's moving laments). What emerges is a clear verdict concerning the inadequacy of the traditional view. It has its truth, but neither can it be pressed. It comes to shipwreck on Job's case.

Chapter 28 represents still another perspective: one can find all kinds of precious metals in the earth, but where is wisdom to be found? God alone knows what and where wisdom is. It is almost as if the author were telling us that there is no real answer to the problems which life poses. The addition of 28:28 about the fear of the Lord is an effort to bring this mystery into traditional understanding, and into the context of Job (cf. 1:8; 2:3), but it cannot gainsay the verdict of *non liquet* ("unclear"), which the poem in chapter 28 presents.

The Elihu narrative is to be understood as a variation on the theme of the three friends. The traditional arguments which he presents are not new; he simply supplies a fresh restatement.

The Yahweh speeches do not give an answer, so much as they prepare Job for the specific response which he will give in 42:5. They serve to change Job's attitude, not to convict him of wrong-doing. They are there to help him put his own miserable and puzzling situation in broader perspective.

The message derived from Job's acclamation in 42:5–6 is an existential one: Job submits to the mysterious ways of the Lord.

Finally, as has been pointed out, the author has not omitted Job's restoration in 42:12–17. For this, too, lies within the provident care of the Lord. Thus, the author has appreciated the complexity of the problem. He has provided no single answer, but he has illuminated brilliantly several aspects of the human condition.

Such a summary of the "message" of the book as we have just presented is necessary, yet somehow deceptive. It does not cover all the facets of life, modern and ancient, which are reflected in this work. Neither does it provide for the *impact* which the book can have, and impact is surely part of the message. Hence we will turn our attention to some aspects of the work that call for greater emphasis than the preceding survey allows.

JOB'S GROWTH

What is to be made of Job's lashing out against God, as he does in several places (7:20–21; 9:22–24; 16:7–17)? Such language contributes to the integrity of the work, and to the humanness of its protagonist. This kind of "prayer" is in harmony with the realistic attitude toward God that is reflected in the psalms of lament. However, what kind of religious attitude underlies Job's outbursts? It is not a question of putting Job down, but one must understand the kind of reasoning that he employs. And it appears that Job's complaints are ultimately based upon the very theory proposed by his friends, and which he argues against! He assumes that God rewards the good, and punishes the evil. That is the way things should be. But the principle is not applicable in his case; something has broken down. He has not sinned, but he is suffering as if he were wicked. He is firm in asserting his own integrity and righteousness, which should obtain from God a better treatment than he has received. Ultimately then, Job is operating in the shadow of the traditional theory of retribution. Because of his own situation he has accused God of injustice, of not allowing him to end his days in prosperity, according to the picture he has drawn in chapter 29:

> Oh, that I were as in the months of old,
> > as in the days when God watched over me;
> when his lamp shown upon my head,
> > and by his light I walked through darkness (29:2-3).

He cannot view his afflication and suffering as anything but punishment from God—a punishment that is misplaced, and hence God is guilty of injustice. This is the inference to be drawn from the Lord's words:

> Will you even put me in the wrong?
> Will you condemn me that you may be justified? (40:8)

On the other hand, Job is perfectly correct in refusing to follow the lead of his friends—that he should repent, admit his sinfulness, and be forgiven and restored by God. This would be to admit that his suffering is a punishment for sin, and he has not sinned. Hence he can assert his righteousness. But he operates on the traditional principle of retribution when he argues with God. He assumed that his suffering is punishment, and he is able to play the other side of the retribution principle: his righteousness should get him something. As R. A. F. MacKenzie remarks: "The correction of the friends' distortion is comparatively simple and can be accomplished by Job himself. His own error is more subtle, and his correction must come from God. In the prologue, he makes no connection between his suffering and divine justice. But that loyal simplicity is not sufficient to refute the friends' accusations, and in maintaining his innocence as though God were denying it, he overvalues it. It is not a bargaining counter; it is not a token he can hold up to God, saying, 'For this, you owe me happiness.' "[15]

The speeches of the Lord constitute a bold attack on Job's apparently reasonable assumption about suffering and injustice. What the speeches lack in sympathy, they make up in mystery. G. K. Chesterton has commented on the mystery in his own paradoxical style: "The refusal of God to explain His design is itself a burning hint of His design. The riddles of God are more satisfying than the solutions of man. . . . God says, in effect, that if there is one fine thing about the world, as far as men are concerned, it is that it cannot be explained. He insists on the inexplicableness of everything: 'Hath the rain a father? . . . Out of whose womb came the ice?' (38:28f.). He goes farther, and insists on the positive and palpable unreason of things: 'Hast thou sent the rain upon the desert where no man is, and upon the wilderness wherein there is no man?' (38:26). God will make man see things, if it is only against the black background of nonentity. God will make Job see a startling universe if He can only do it by making Job see an idiotic universe. To startle man God becomes for an instant a blasphemer; one might almost say that God becomes for an instant an atheist. He unrolls before Job a long panorama of created things, the horse, the eagle, the raven, the wild ass, the peacock, the ostrich, the crocodile. He so describes each of them that it sounds like a monster walking in the sun. The whole is a sort of psalm or rhapsody of the sense of wonder. The maker of all things is astonished at the things He has Himself made."[16] Chesterton has overstated the case for the Lord's speeches. But one cannot overlook the change that they produce upon Job. Even if he might yearn for the days of his prosperity, he has now a vision of God that puts them in the shadow. He gives the Lord freedom to act.

GOD'S FREEDOM

The history of several religions has revealed a firm tendency among human beings: the restriction of divinity. If God is not made in the image of man, at least his liberty is limited. Humans seem fundamentally unable to tolerate a God who is truly free. He must act according to the definition laid down by them. Human concepts of justice and love become the framework, even the cage, of divinity. This is true of those who profess allegiance to the God of the Bible.

The very understandable desire for certainty and security leads to a description of a God that is firm and reliable—and thereby void of mystery.

The biblical tradition itself reflects this constant effort to control God, to make him accountable. But within the tradition there is also the idea of the *Deus absconditus* ("hidden God"; cf. Isa. 45:15, "Truly, thou are a God who hidest thyself"). It is Israel's glory that the struggle for divine freedom is so honestly portrayed in the pages of the Old Testament. The divine soliloquy in Hosea 11:5–9 is an example of how the Lord breaks through the limitations that might be readily placed upon his mercy. He decrees punishment for Israel (11:5–7), and then he cries out:

> How can I give you up, O Ephraim!
>> How can I hand you over, O Israel! . . .
> My heart recoils within me,
>> my compassion grows warm and tender.
> I will not execute my fierce anger,
>> I will not again destroy Ephraim;
> for I am God and not man,
>> the Holy One in your midst,
>> and I will not come to destroy (Hos. 11:8–9).

Here the Lord breaks the bonds which "justice" imposes upon the covenantal relationship with Israel. He will have mercy on whom he will have mercy: "I will be gracious to whom I will be gracious, and will show mercy on whom I will show mercy" (Exod. 33:19; Rom. 9:15).

This insight into the mystery of divine freedom seems too dangerous for human beings. It is almost as if human recognition of wrong becomes itself a barrier to the understanding of divine mercy. Israel's own failures abetted this view. The Deuteronomic theologians put it in black-and-white terms: choose life—or death (Deut. 30:15–20). They structured the Deuteronomistic history (Joshua through Kings) on this principle. Since the destruction of Jerusalem and the exile proved that Israel's choice was for death, Israel's history is portrayed in this light. Even here, not all hope is lost (there is a hint of a future in 2 Kings 25:27–30), but it takes a tremendous effort by an unknown prophet of the exile to persuade the people that Yahweh will once again show mercy (Isa. 40–49). Robert Frost is right when he has the Lord refer to the Deuteronomist in a dialogue with Job. To Job's inquiry about heaven, God replies:

> Yes, by and by. But first a larger matter.
> I've had you on my mind a thousand years
> To thank you someday for the way you helped me
> Establish once for all the principle
> There's no connection man can reason out
> Between his just deserts and what he gets.
> Virtue may fail and wickedness succeed.
> 'Twas a great demonstration we put on. . . .
> But it was of the essence of the trial
> You shouldn't understand it at the time.
> It had to seem unmeaning to have meaning.
> And it came out all right. I have no doubt
> You realize by now the part you played
> To stultify the Deuteronomist
> And change the tenor of religious thought.
> My thanks are to you for releasing me
> From moral bondage to the human race. . . .
> I had to prosper good and punish evil.
> You changed all that. You set me free to reign.
> > Robert Frost, "A Masque of Reason"[17]

Individually and collectively, the justice of the Lord was seen as operating in tandem with human response. This understanding is at the heart of any "I–thou" relationship, but it can fail to allow for the freedom and the mystery of suffering inherent in the human condition. Against this background one can readily appreciate the thrust of the Book of Job. It is a stark confrontation with a mechanical view of divine response. Ecclesiastes followed in the same path, and even more drastically. For him there is simply no way of making sense out of life. One can not understand the "work of God" (Eccles. 8:17): "whether it is love or hate man does not know . . . since one fate comes to all, to the righteous and the wicked, to the good and the evil . . ." (9:1–2). Although the Book of Job is less trenchant in expression, it affirms the same lesson of divine freedom.

JOB'S FAITH

In view of the charge of blasphemy that is so easily levelled against Job, there is need to underscore the profound faith that animates him throughout the debate. It is not a faith that draws on the consoling truths of Israel's history, such as the motifs that are so frequently found in the Book of Psalms. It is a faith that accepts God as creator, but also as involved personally in his creation; faith in a God who does not tolerate wrongdoers (13:16), whence Job derives hope for his own hearing; a God who controls all that occurs, whence Job holds him accountable (chaps. 12, 16, 19) a God who is present, yet absent (chap. 23).

Job's witness to God as creator is expressed in the hymnic style that is characteristic of biblical praise of the creator (Pss. 103, 104, 147; Amos 4:13; 5:18–19). He shows himself to be as knowledgeable of creation theology as the Lord himself in chapters 39—41:

> He is wise in heart, and mighty in strength
> —who has hardened himself against him,
> and succeeded?—
> he who removes mountains, and they know it not,
> when he overturns them in his anger;
> who shakes the earth out of its place,
> and its pillars tremble;
> who commands the sun, and it does not rise;
> who seals up the stars;
> who alone stretched out the heavens,
> and trampled the waves of the sea;
> who made the Bear and Orion,
> the Pleiades and the chambers of the south;
> who does great things beyond understanding,
> and marvelous things without number (Job 9:4–10).

But might does not constitute right. Job's very acknowledgement of his creator makes it all the more difficult to deal with him: "he passes me by, and I see him not" (9:11). Job has experienced the under side of God:

> I was at ease, and he broke me asunder;
> he seized me by the neck and dashed me to pieces;

he set me up as his target,
    his archers surround me.
He slashes open my kidneys and does not spare;
    he pours out my gall on the ground.
He breaks me with breach upon breach;
    he runs upon me like a warrior (16:12–14).

One must not look for a logical development of faith in Job. In fact, he has as much faith when he opens with the lament of chapter 3 as when he closes with his challenge in chapter 31. The reader may mark high points and low points in this odyssey. It is precisely this wavering that makes for the verisimilitude of the work. Job emerges as a person of genuine faith *because* he persists in quarreling with God to the end. The formalism which prohibits an honest confrontation with God is not part of biblical faith. The price to be paid for faith may be excruciating, but the relationship itself is a real one, not a facade of observances, or timorous submission. This is why Job is correct in his bold appeal to God's "better self," to the one he knows will vindicate him:

Even now, behold, my witness is in heaven,
    and he that vouches for me is on high.
My friends scorn me;
    my eyes pour out tears to God,
that he would maintain the right of a man with God,
    like that of a man with his neighbor (16:19–21).

Job refuses to believe that the God he knows is other than just. He might taunt such a God, and even encourage him to use his power to destroy him, but "this would be my consolation. . . . for I have not denied the words of the Holy One" (6:10). This resilient faith left room for even a certain sympathy with God's personal involvement with him. Job utters the impossible wish of respite in Sheol. Even then, God is not easily free of his own creature:

Oh that thou wouldest hide me in Sheol,
    that thou wouldest conceal me until thy wrath be past,
    that thou wouldest appoint me a set time, and remember me!

If a man die, shall he live again?
   All the days of my service I would wait,
   till my release should come.
Thou wouldest call, and I would answer thee;
   thou wouldest long for the work of thy hands (14:13–15).

The intensity, as well as the fluctuation, of Job's faith is beautifully described in chapter 23. He gives up none of the need he feels to defend himself. If only he could confront God, he feels confident that he would recognize his loyalty. He no longer gives in to his earlier doubts about putting his case before God (9:14–15). There is always the divine power to contend with, but he would give Job a hearing (23:6). But where to find him?

Behold, I go forward, but he is not there;
   and backward, but I cannot perceive him;
on the left hand I seek him, but I cannot behold him;
   I turn to the right hand, but I cannot see him (23:8–9).

The theme of God's hiddenness will, of course, be met by the awefulness of his appearance in the theophany of chapter 39. The absence of God is too much for Job to bear. Even though God knows his integrity (23:10–12), Job unfortunately cannot think he will reverse his attitude. So Job trembles:

Therefore I am terrified at his presence;
   when I consider, I am in dread of him.
God has made my heart faint;
   the Almighty has terrified me (23:15–16).

NOTES

1. Martin Luther, *Word and Sacrament I*, Luther's Works, vol. 35, ed. E. Theodore Bachmann, trans. Charles M. Jacobs (Philadelphia: Fortress, 1960), pp. 255–256.
2. Karl Rahner, *More Recent Writings*, trans. Kevin Smyth. Theological Investigations, vol. 4 (Baltimore: Helicon, 1966) p. 363.
3. Walter Brueggemann, "From Hurt to Joy, From Death to Life," and Claus Westermann, "The Role of the Lament in the Theology of the Old Testament," *Interpretation* 28, no. 1 (1974): 3–38.
4. Walter Brueggemann, "From Hurt to Joy, From Death to Life," *Interpretation* 28, no. 1 (1974): 18.
5. Sigmund Mowinckel, *The Psalms in Israel's Worship*, trans. D.R. Ap-Thomas (Nashville: Abingdon, 1967) vol. 1, p. 51.
6. Claus Westermann, "The Role of the Lament in the Theology of the Old Testament," *Interpretation* 28, no. 1 (1974): 20–38.
7. Walter Brueggemann, "The Formfulness of Grief," *Interpretation* 31, no. 3 (1977): 263–275.
8. John H. Reumann, "Psalm 22 at the Cross," *Interpretation* 28, no. 1 (1974): 39–58.
9. Dietrich Bonhoeffer, *Letters and Papers from Prison*, ed. Eberhard Bethge, trans. Reginald H. Fuller (New York: Macmillan, 1962) pp. 103–104.
10. R. A. F. MacKenzie, "Job," *The Jerome Biblical Commentary* (Englewood Cliffs: Prentice-Hall, 1968) 31:93.
11. Patrick W. Skehan, *Studies in Israelite Poetry and Wisdom*, The Catholic Biblical Quarterly Monograph Series 1 (Washington: Catholic Biblical Association of America, 1971) pp. 114–123.
12. Marvin H. Pope, *Job*, The Anchor Bible (Garden City: Doubleday, and Co. 1973) vol. 15, p. xxxi.
13. J. William Whedbee, "The Comedy of Job," *Semeia 7: Studies in the Book of Job* (Missoula, Montana: Scholars Press, 1977) pp. 1–39.
14. Marvin H. Pope, *op. cit.*, p. lxxxii.
15. R. A. F. MacKenzie, *op. cit.*, 31:6.
16. W. H. Auden, ed., *G. K. Chesterton: A Selection From His Non-Fictional Prose* (London: Faber and Faber, 1970) pp. 153–154.

SELECTED BIBLIOGRAPHY

PSALMS

BARTH, CHRISTOPH. *Introduction to the Psalms*, trans. R. A. Wilson (New York: Scribner, 1966).

BRUEGGEMANN, WALTER. "From Hurt to Joy, From Death to Life," *Interpretation* 28 (1974) 3–19; "The Formfulness of Grief," *Interpretation* 31 (1977) 263–275.

GUNKEL, HERMANN. *The Psalms,* trans. Thomas M. Horner. Facet Books, Biblical Series, 19 (Philadelphia: Fortress, 1967).

KRAUS, HANS-JOACHIM. *Psalmen*. Biblischer Kommentar Altes Testament (Neukirchen: Neukirchener Verlag, 1960).

MACKENZIE, R. A. F. *The Book of Psalms*. Old Testament Reading Guide 23 (Collegeville, Minn.: Liturgical Press, 1967).

MOWINCKEL, SIGMUND. *The Psalms in Israel's Worship*, trans. D. R. Ap-Thomas (Nashville: Abingdon, 1967).

MURPHY, ROLAND E. "Psalms," *The Jerome Biblical Commentary* (Englewood Cliffs, N.J.: Prentice-Hall, 1968) 569–602.

VON RAD, GERHARD. *Old Testament Theology*, trans. D. M. G. Stalker (New York: Harper & Row, 1962).

RINGGREN, HELMER. *The Faith of the Psalmists* (Philadelphia: Fortress, 1963)

WEISER, ARTUR *The Psalms,* trans. Herbert Hartwell (London: SMC, 1962).

WESTERMANN, CLAUS. "The Role of the Lament in the Theology of the Old Testament," *Interpretation* 28 (1974) 20–38.

JOB

ANDERSEN, FRANCIS I. *Job*. Tyndale Old Testament Commentaries (Leicester: Inter-Variety Press, 1976).

DHORME, EDOUARD. *A Commentary on the Book of Job*, trans. Harold Knight (London: Nelson, 1967).

GORDIS, ROBERT. *The Book of God and Man: A Study of Job* (Univ. of Chicago Press, 1965).

MACKENZIE, R. A. F. "Job," *The Jerome Biblical Commentary* (Englewood Cliffs, N.J.: Prentice-Hall, 1968) 511–533.

POLZIN, ROBERT; ROBERTSON, DAVID, eds. *Semeia 7: Studies in the Book of Job* (Missoula, Montana: Scholars Press, 1977).

POPE, MARVIN. *Job*. Anchor Bible 15 (New York: Doubleday, 1973).

PRITCHARD, JAMES B., ed. *Ancient Near Eastern Texts (ANET)*. Supplement, third edition (Princeton: Princeton University Press, 1969).

VON RAD, GERHARD. *Wisdom in Israel* (Nashville: Abingdon, 1972).

94